EVERYDAY LEADERSHIP SERIES #1: ENGAGEMENT

TAKE THE LEAD:

Full-Throttle Engagement
Powered by Coaching

Leta M. Beam

To: Lisa ~
Be better & different
each ╫╫ day!!

HUGO HOUSE PUBLISHERS

Warmly,
Leta

Take the Lead: *Full-Throttle Engagement Powered by Coaching*

© 2012 Leta Beam. All Rights Reserved

ISBN: 978-1-936449-18-7

Library of Congress Control Number: 2012934097

Limits of Liability and Disclaimer of Warranty

The author and publisher shall not be liable for your misuse of this material. This book is strictly for informational and educational purposes.

Warning—Disclaimer

The purpose of this book is to educate and entertain. The author and/or publisher do not guarantee that anyone following these techniques, suggestions, tips, ideas, or strategies will become successful. The author and/or publisher shall have neither liability nor responsibility to anyone with respect to any loss or damage caused, or alleged to be caused, directly or indirectly by the information contained in this book.

Cover Design & Interior Layout: Ronda Taylor, www.taylorbydesign.com

Cover Illustration: Chandra Wheeler

Published by:

Hugo House Publishers, Ltd.
Englewood, CO
Austin, TX
(877) 700-0616
www.HugoHousePublishers.com

A Very Special Permission and Acknowledgement:

My leadership and business coaching enterprise, Vantage International, and, more specifically, this book, *Take The Lead*, would not have been possible had it not been for the content rich curriculum of Comprehensive Coaching U (www.coachinstitute. com), the practical business applications intentionally offered through that community and the superior coaching and leadership of its founder, Terri Levine. The philosophical approach and skills offered through Terri Levine (www.terrilevine. com) are embedded in the DNA of my business and all aspects of my work. The coaching skills offered in *Take The Lead* are rooted in The Coaching Institute tradition. While I have built upon and refined my initial coaching education over the past twelve years, it is important to acknowledge the pivotal role that it played in shaping my own body of work. For additional information on Terri and the Coaching Institute, please visit both www.TerriLevine.com and www.CoachInstitute.com.

Permissions:

The following quotes, graphs, and pictures are used with permission of the authors:

For the graph and picture in chapter 1: © Daniel H. Pink and from *A Whole New Mind*. Figure 3.1.

For the quote on 212 degrees: © Sam Parker, *212° the extra degree°*. (www.GiveMore. com)

Marianne Williamson's quote: © Marianne Williamson, *A Return to Love*.

Five Levels of Right Questions: © Kurt and Patricia Wright. *Breaking the Rules: Removing Obstacles to Effortless High Performance* (1998).

All quotes from Ben and Roz Zander. © Benjamin Zander and Rosamund Stone Zander. *The Art of Possibility*. New York: Penguin Books, 2002.

Traditional Versus Engaged Organizations in chapter 2 and the Communication Assessment in chapter 6: @Annette Cremo, Ph.D., President, Performance Plus Training & Consulting.

All references to Stephen R. Covey's *The 7 Habits of Highly Effective People*, copyright 1984 and renewed in 2004 by Stephen R. Covery, are use with permission of the FranklinCovey Co.

Dedication

This book is dedicated to my Daddy, Frank Bansky (1916-2011) in recognition of his tenacity, resilience, and unswerving optimism.

One of his favorite sayings, "It doesn't cost a thing to smile," has become one of my dearest mantras. The spirit of connection and good will that is captured in this quote is woven into the fabric of my life and work.

Raging Appreciations

Thanksgiving Day comes around 365 times each year for me. That's because I begin almost every day of my life with what I call, raging appreciation. I think of ten things for which I am particularly grateful in the first moments of that day. Sometimes those things are really huge, such as great health; others are smaller, such as a fine night's sleep in a warm bed. And some are just plain silly—the crazy antics of my three cats! Sometimes my raging appreciations make me smile, laugh, and even cry.

What I've come to know wholeheartedly as a result of this everyday practice is that what I express gratitude for is far less important than feeding the habit of simply being appreciative for the magic and abundance that is in my life and never taking my blessings for granted.

It is therefore with great joy that I share with each of you my raging appreciation surrounding the creation and publication of *Take the Lead*. This amazing journey has been filled with messengers, teachers, cheerleaders, coaches, and success partners who genuinely cared enough about my success and who were committed enough to reshaping our workplaces by fanning the flame of the passion that I routinely feel for everyday leadership and full-throttle engagement. Every one of these extraordinary individuals is a role model who leads from their seats and practices everyday leadership with gusto, grit, and fervor.

In particular:

I offer a humble and sincere thank you to my clients and colleagues, who strongly and relentlessly encouraged me to put fingers to keypad and capture the transformational message that every single person in every single workplace is a leader.

I owe a deep and loving thank you to my fiancé, Jim. First, for lifting me up with his love and inviting my very best self to come out and play each day. And second, for expressing ongoing and unswerving belief in me and for helping me to create the time, space, energy, and spirit to "listen to the voices in my head and heart" that told me to deliver this message in a way that lots of people would understand.

I offer a profound and deep-seated thank you to Terri Levine for her inspiring business coaching and her like-minded belief in the awesome potential that coach-leadership has to transform who we are and how we are together at work.

I proudly offer a heartfelt thank you to my amazing daughter, Shannon, for her calm certainty and nonchalant expectation that, of course, *Take the Lead* would be a wildly successful book! How could it be otherwise!

I extend a warm and very personal thank you to my senior editor and publisher, Dr. Patricia Ross, who played the pivotal role of alchemist, helping me to turn my everyday thoughts and common words into something special by cracking open a portal to my creativity and settling for nothing less than my very best work.

Finally, I am so thankful for the thousands of "everyday leaders" whose paths have crossed with mine for inspiring me and refreshing in me the belief that not only is full-throttle engagement possible, it is who and what we are intended to be in our workplace communities.

To each of you, you have touched my heart and lifted my spirit in more ways than you can possibly imagine. For that, I will always be supremely grateful.

Contents

"*If your actions inspire others to dream more, learn more, do more and become more, YOU ARE A LEADER.***"**

—John Quincy Adams

Backstory

*The End Game: Your Seat **IS** a Power Seat*

How much greatness are we willing to grant people?
—Ben & Roz Zander

*How **big** are you willing to play to*
help make your organization great?
—Leta Beam

I remember the first time, as a young, twenty-something professional, I snuck an unauthorized peek at the executive conference room of my company. Top floor. Panoramic view. No detail spared. You know the kind of room I mean.

In the center of the room was a huge table, impressive in size and quality, with maybe twenty equally imposing chairs. I was simultaneously intimidated, awed, and excited. I imagined all of the decisions made around that table and the power wielded from those chairs. I naively thought that the success of our organization rested with the power brokers whose butts occupied those big, plush seats. I believed at the time that the people occupying those seats were somehow different from me and everyone else in the company. They were special. Practically anointed.

At the time I really believed that whoever sat in those chairs had to be smarter or more insightful than me—more important, more valued than me or my colleagues. I was sure they knew how to do my job better than I did. They were "rock stars," or so it seemed because they were making all of the decisions.

I vowed then and there to find my way back to that table and into one of those chairs. Only then, I thought, could I truly consider myself one of the "leaders."

Fast forward twenty-five or thirty years. Now as a leadership and business coach, I would love to say that this way of thinking and behaving is laughable, but I can't. The fact is that some organizations and some professionals remain stuck in that same place I was, thinking that there must be someone more important, more capable, more responsible for the success of the company than they.

How many people are unfulfilled, disillusioned, or just kinda numb at work? Maybe even cynical? You know who I'm talking about. Those people who are waiting to be told what to do. Beaten up instead of upbeat. Either looking elsewhere for a chance to be at their best or resigned to passively accepting "the way things are around here."

These types of people in the workplace are all too predictable, and they tend to drag the rest down. This is because most of the workforce around the globe still functions in something I call "dysfunctional comfort." It means that we keep doing things the same old way even though we recognize that it doesn't come close to us at our best. We keep doing those things because they are a familiar habit. That's dysfunctional because the very idea that "this is just how things are meant to be" in the workplace is a lie. A big fat one.

The old way of being together in the workplace doesn't work any-more. Most of you know what I mean by *old* way...

- That "I'm the boss and I have all the answers, so when I want your opinion, I'll give it to you" model or...
- The "woe is me, I'm just a _____ (fill in the blank with your position or work description) and what I think doesn't matter" approach or...
- The "I know what's best for you and this organization" speech or...

- The "Let them fix all of these problems; after all that's why they get paid the big bucks" perspective or maybe....
- The "I've tried and tried to improve things around here and nothing ever changes, so I'm just giving up" whine.

And most of you, on some level, also know that this same-old, same-old way of organizing ourselves at work and conducting business not only just isn't cutting it, it's wrong headed. Unfortunately, here's the hard fact of the matter: the longer we cling to the old way, the harder it will be to co-create a healthy, productive and satisfying environment.

The workforce, especially in developed, mature countries, has outgrown the old industrial model of manager/worker which was far too much like that of a parent and child. It's the model that fosters same-old, same-old thinking, where leaders are only found in corner offices, executive conference rooms, or behind doors that have the words "director," "manager," or "president," on them.

As a leadership and business coach, I no longer want to help my colleagues and clients to simply get better and better at a model that is wrong-er and wrong-er. I have a burning desire to help them grab hold of new ideas and learn how to take responsibility for their position at work, no matter what position that is. I want everyone in the organization to be on fire about what they do, taking responsibility not only for their individual duties but for the goals of the entire organization: this results in everyone being fully engaged, thriving, and fulfilled by their jobs instead of looking at the clock, waiting for 5:00 p.m. when they can check out. That's the central idea behind the series "Everyday Leadership," and that is why the first book in this series is titled *Take the Lead*. I want to challenge everyone in all organizations: for profit, not-for-profit, governmental, private, public, small, medium, and large to step up, take charge, and take the lead in their organizations; create healthy, vibrant working environments and take pride in what they are accomplishing both personally and collectively within their organization as a whole.

Your Seat Is a Power Seat

Several years ago, Bill Ford told the employees at Ford Motor Company, "We can't play the same old game the same old way." He was right. It is my strong belief that what got us all here to our current level of success will *not* take us into the future. But that begs a question: what does the future look like?

I think it is one where we, as a global community, herald a new age of meaning, contribution, innovation, and prosperity through workplace engagement. To create that, we must recognize that:

- We are a collection of *adults*, working together toward a shared vision, mission, and value system. We must forever banish the parent-child model from the workplace.
- Each one of us is completely responsible for our duties and our contribution. No excuses.
- Each of us is not only responsibility for our duties; we also *own* the overall success of our organization as well. That means that we make it our business to clearly understand how what we do fits with what our fellow employees do and how it all comes together to help the people who use our products and services.
- We are our sister's and our brother's keeper. We've got to care about other people's success as much as we do about our own. We need to accept responsibility for building and growing ourselves and each other.

There are some key words in this list that I just gave you, words that I'm going to come back to time and again because they are the backbone of what it means to be an everyday leader, strong words like "responsibility," "owning," and "engagement." The whole idea behind what I teach every day to businesses large and small is that *each one of us is a leader in our organization.*

Leading is NOT someone else's job. Regardless of title, position, and salary or grade level, you are not *just* a ___! You need to get right with the fact that you are a VIL (Very Important Leader). You are an expert at what you do all day. This is vastly different from and more than just being "good at" what you do. You must choose to lead from wherever you fit in the organization.

I call it leading from your seat, and it comes from the idea that Ben & Rose Zander illustrated so masterfully in their book, *The Art of Possibility*. They talk about how, in an orchestra, every musician is assigned a "chair." Take the violin section. There are two sections, and each violinist is assigned a chair: first section first chair, first section second chair, and so on. Now, this is what I love about this idea: even though it would seem that the violinist that sits in the first chair in the first section of the orchestra is the most important, he isn't! Every "chair" in the orchestra has an important job. If the second section sixth violinist thinks he isn't important and therefore doesn't tune his instrument or doesn't follow the conductor's instructions, the whole orchestra sounds out of tune. The person who isn't playing to his best ability or isn't taking responsibility for his part in the overall goal of the orchestra sticks out like the sour notes he is producing. In a well-tuned orchestra, each "chair" in an orchestra is a power chair because every instrument contributes to the overall harmony of the sound.[1]

However, orchestras do not traditionally think of themselves in those terms. Like in the dysfunctional world of same-old, same-old in business, orchestras in the past have been painfully hierarchical with the conductor often applying a "my way or the highway" leadership style. However, the point the Zanders ultimately make in their book is that an orchestra performs far better when the conductor recognizes that "each chair is a power chair," and thus welcomes suggestions for better ways to interpret and play the musical piece because it comes from the musicians who are doing the playing! The success of this approach is beautifully captured by one of the talented young musicians who worked with the Zanders who experienced this "new age" of leadership:

> *"...Sitting at the back of the cello section when I have always sat at the front, was the hardest thing I've done in a long while....Your shine inspired me to believe that I have the force of personality to power the section from wherever I sit and I believe that I led the concert from the 11th chair...From this day on, I will be leading*

every section in which I sit—whichever seat." Georgina, cellist, New Zealand National Youth Orchestra.[2]

Georgina gets it! She is a VIL! Just like her, *you are a leader* no matter where your seat is in your organization. Your seat belongs at the leadership table because you are a powerful force in determining just how successful your organization is going to be. Your seat IS a power seat.

Now, I must pause here and clarify what this type of leadership doesn't mean. It does not mean that anyone can go "rogue." It does not mean that there is no hierarchy, and it definitely doesn't mean that you start doing your boss's job or take over a colleague's responsibilities.

But here's the best part: once you recognize the fundamental aspect of the role *you* play in your organization, wouldn't it be exhilarating (I'm talking goose bumps here) to think about what it would look like and feel like for *everyone* to view themselves as leading from their seat at work? This is what I think would happen:

1. You know your job inside and out.

2. Every day, you routinely ask yourself, "Am I doing what needs to be done?"

3. Every day you look for ways to do it differently and better. You prepare suggestions and ideas for how to make things better and you share them with others to get feedback.

4. Throughout the day, you take stock of how things are going and what you can do to be more useful and effective.

5. You know what others do and how what you do blends with their "stuff' for the good of the organization.

6. You see yourself as an owner of the organization. It does not fall to someone else to make this a great place to work and really, really successful. It's your job.

7. You do your work well, creatively, with grit and gusto. You bring your best self to work. No excuses.

8. You acknowledge that you may only have part of the picture and others may have ideas that are both different from and better than yours.

9. You avoid constant comparisons of the type and amount of your contribution versus another team member. You are only in charge of you and you choose to model leadership behavior.

10. You actively help others to be their best. And you give them permission to help you by opening yourself to constructive feedback from those around you.

11. You make it a habit to applaud and support others' efforts to make positive changes and improvements in their work.

12. You listen with a cooperative ear to proposed organizational changes that will require you to change, too. You listen for opportunities to be even better at your duties.

13. You are regularly tuned in to your self-talk and your emotions, so that you continually choose those constructive thoughts and feelings that will reinforce new habits and move you and your organization forward.

Let me tell you a story about someone who really "gets" shared leadership. Her name is Martha and she works at the supermarket where I do my food shopping. And every single day, she is leading from her seat in the organization even though I am positive that she does not have the title of "store manager." In fact, her official title understates the huge contribution she makes to the success of the store. She sees herself as personally in charge of helping you to find every single grocery item that you need so that you leave a happy shopper. She bends your ear about how proud she is to work at this store, how fortunate we all are to have so much food that we can't find what we want, and about how she loves her job. She has made it her business to know where every item is located. I have never known her to call someone else to get the job done. She hangs in there until she has the item; and if the store doesn't carry it, she suggests a substitute or finds one at some other store. And I *have never* seen her as anything less than joyful at work!

There are more and more Marthas in workplaces, and they almost always share a common benefit that comes naturally from leading from their seat. For something remarkable, maybe even magical, happens as you begin to lead from your seat at work. I see it every day. You are uplifted. The day is less stressful and more meaningful. You feel as though you are making a difference more often. You're more creative. You feel pumped more often. You have more fun, see the lighter side of things, and time flies by. Equally important, others are inspired by your everyday example.

The whole purpose of this book is to help you develop a way to become a leader from your seat, and I will get into the particulars shortly. For now, I want to give you another benefit to living and working this way. As you begin to shift and change, you may begin to experience lots of interactions differently. For example, you will take special notice, as I did recently, when the front desk representative at the Comfort Inn came out from behind her desk to help me get all of my business materials to my room in one trip. I travel frequently to speak, facilitate educational programs, and coach teams and individuals in organizations across the US and beyond; and I interact with many hospitality professionals as part of that experience. This particular front- desk clerk could have made me wait for someone else or let me struggle on my own. But no, she took the time to help me. *And*, because I stay at this Comfort Inn somewhat frequently this front- line employee remembered that I liked to exercise and told me about the new equipment they'd acquired. If that wasn't enough, she asked if I wanted her to show me how to use it. Finally, she thanked me for being *her* guest. It didn't matter that this person was "just" a clerk. She sees herself as an integral part of the overall success of that Comfort Inn, and that decision on her part translated into one happy guest, *me*!

Let's face it: WOWing customers, patients, clients, guests, etc., is an end goal of pretty much all organizations. And as I find more and more examples of people leading from their seats, I'm thrilled to notice the effect it has on me as a client or a customer. Everyday leaders save customers time and money. This happened to me recently, when a warehouse worker told his boss that he had a suggestion on how to make our carpet purchase and installation both cheaper and easier. His idea was brilliant; the manager graciously got out of his way and allowed him to take the lead and we got a terrific deal! Will we shop there in the future? You bet.

Everyday leaders make it their business to develop strong, caring relationships so that customers can't help but feel special. Everyday leaders understand that who they are, what they do, and how they do it translates directly to the customer's experience.

Power your organization from wherever you sit!

But great customer relations are only part of the payoff to being everyday leaders. It's what happens inside an organization that fires me up.

We *all* urgently need to start thinking, feeling, believing, and acting very differently than ever before. That's the end game. And it doesn't matter whether you hold an office worker, staff member, middle manager, or C-Suite position in your organization. It is no longer enough to show up for work wearing blinders, content to do your *j-o-b*—that set of duties that you narrowly define and too often dread performing.

If you are among the professionals who continue to wait for someone else to take charge of problem solving and the overall success and well-being of your organization, a condition often called learned helplessness, then this is a wake-up call!

Whether we choose to acknowledge it or not, most of us have a significant amount of influence over the results that we produce at work. If you do not cultivate the bravery and the ability to contribute your leadership now, you will be less and less of a fit as organizations reimagine themselves.

Think of this as a leadership dare! I dare you to play big and let your greatness shine in your organization. I dare you to *Take the Lead*!

Now I want you to stop reading for a moment and really take a look at the cover of this book. What do you see? A rendering of a conference table, the very same around which the movers and shakers in a business gather. But what's different? Who do you suppose is sitting *at this* leadership table?

The chairs aren't all the plush "power seat" chairs. They are the everyday chairs in which we all sit. Instead of a group of suits sitting at the leadership table making all the decisions for your company, can you picture all types of people holding all sorts of positions sitting around a table, visioning, brain-storming, making brilliant decisions, and creating innovative solutions to your organization's challenges? Taking action, Taking responsibility. Taking charge. Now, look at the chairs again. Do you recognize your chair among those pictured?

There is a critical imperative with which we are faced today: if we want to continue to be a success in business, then we must re-define leadership. We need to invite everyone at all levels of any business to come take their seat at the leadership table.

The Problem:

Same-Old, Same-Old Thinkin'

The End Game is all about a call to action for everyone in an organization to work together, shooting for a different outcome. I started *Take the Lead* that way because I think one of the same-old, same-old ways of thinking is to bludgeon the reader with all the problems they're facing so that they're ready to face the solution when it's presented.

If you got anything from what you've just read, I hope that it is the idea that I'm not about keeping the same-old, same-old just because it's worked in the past. Business as usual will *not* get us where we need to be in the future. Each and every one of us must come to a new understanding of the outcome that will make our organizations successful and wholeheartedly participate in achieving it. Taking the lead, finding out what it looks and feels like to lead from your seat, why it's more important than ever and to get moving in that direction—that's the goal of this book. But in order to get there, we need to step back and look at the problem we're working to solve around that goal.

So the first question to start with is, why are so many people disillusioned or disconnected at work? Statistics gathered from national surveys across different industries reveal that nearly three-fourths of American workers are ***not engaged*** at work. That means that they're doing only the minimum of what's required and giving very little extra in terms of innovation, caring, and ownership. But here's the scary one: 17 percent are ***actively disengaged*** according to a Gallop poll.[3] In the Towers & Perrin 2005 Global Workforce Survey, only 14 percent reported that they were highly engaged at work. Similar, but smaller studies have put that number as low as 3 percent.[4]

One of the reasons why we're so disengaged at work is that most of us continue to operate under what is often called the "command and control" model, a leftover from the factory mindset of the Industrial Age. Because it delivered some dazzling capabilities during the twentieth century, and because it was the only model that many people in business had ever known, it has hung on throughout much of the Information Age, including the technology-centered era that has spanned the last four decades up to the present.

However, I'm not the only one who is beginning to realize that being stuck in the "old way" has also trapped us in a tangle of "wicked problems," as Horst Rittel calls them. These are the problems that feel so persistent, so pervasive, and so slippery that they seem insolvable. Do any of these wicked problems sound familiar to you?

- Either feeling the need to be the parent or resenting being treated like a child at work.
- Feeling deflated or frustrated because, at the end of the day, you wonder if what you did that day really mattered or made a difference in your organization.
- Being micromanaged by someone who doesn't have a good idea of what you do and how it gets done and, as a result, having to do "fake work" to keep them happy.
- Being handed goals instead of being asked to create them.
- Getting caught up in turf wars.
- Being so consumed with checking items off your task list that you lose sight of the vision and mission of your organization and the meaning of your work.

Consider the following patient experience that illustrates how the old way of being together plays out every day in health care systems in our country:

A patient is looking for help in managing their diabetes. They follow their insurance company's direction and contact the call center to get an appointment with a doctor. The call center representative knows how to use the scheduling software masterfully and wants to be helpful, but she can't because she does not have full access to this doctor's calendar and does not have authority to schedule this appointment after 5:00 p.m., the time preferred by the patient. She tells the patient that someone in the doctor's office will have to call her back because she only handles incoming calls. She sends an email to the administrative professional in the doctor's office. She, in turn, checks with the physician to get permission to schedule an evening appointment because it's an exception to procedure. The physician is focused on clinical care issues and sees this as an unwelcome distraction. In his mind, he is there to take great care of patients when they walk through the clinic doors, and someone else needs to handle the business end of things. He is really good at his job, but he doesn't see this as part of it. Frustrated, the admin in the doctor's office tries in vain to work around the doctor to accommodate the patient. Three days later, she calls the patient to inform her that the next evening appointment is in three months—no exceptions.

Think about how you felt when you read the story about Martha in the End Game, and how you feel now after reading about this situation. It begs the question: What would a "Martha" do in the same set of circumstances?

Here's the problem in a nutshell: even though all three of these professionals may have performed their job duties satisfactorily, each of them seems to be suffering from a bad case of tunnel thinking. There is little evidence of passion for taking on full responsibility for the patient's overall experience.

Or, consider this recent telephone conversation that I had with a customer service representative from a major telecommunications provider:

"...I really wish that I could help you. The other representative routed you to the wrong area. You need to talk to billing. They have their own separate system so I can't even see your account. I can transfer you over there but we don't do warm transfers anymore where I stay on the line to explain your situation to the next person. You'll have to sit in the queue and then tell them what you just told me. Good luck and have a nice day."

I bet that all of the folks that I spoke to during that call (BTW, there were five!) were good at their *j-o-b-s*. But do you think they enjoy going to work? Are they truly engaged? Worse, and unfortunately for me, none of them saw my satisfaction as their individual responsibility.

Lack of engagement is the overall challenge, but to really tackle it head on, we've got to drill a little bit deeper and prospect for the smaller problems that contribute to it. Here's one of them, one that bugs me to no end: these same-old, same-old habits of thinking, feeling and acting run so deep that not only do we just accept that "this is the way it is" or "this is the way it *has to be*," but in fact the old model actually sets us up to be average rather than brilliant. One of my clients had a "aha!" moment and recognized this toxic pattern in her workplace. Her truth was that she and her teammates took solace in mediocrity. Now that's a powerful insight.

The old "command and control" model actually sets us up to work on autopilot. Think about it. It says, "Do what you're told, no more and no less. Be predictable. The boss knows best. Many of you can't be trusted with making decisions. You are lazy and need to be watched." In this model, we're not really supposed to think, be creative, or solve problems. It is so tempting to become discouraged, feel powerless, disconnected, disappointed—you get the picture.

How many times have you heard that "Work isn't supposed to be fun or joyful. That's why it's called work!" …or… "Everyone hates their work. It's not just me!"

That's a wicked problem.

One of my favorite things to do as a business coach when I am visiting a new client organization for the first time is to simply blend in to the flow of the place. I visit the cafeteria, walk the hallways, and chat with lots of different types of people. One question that I love to ask is: "Who's in charge of the success of this place?"

What do you think the most common answer is? What would your team mates say if I were at your organization asking that question? The typical answer is still "the boss," "the higher ups," or the more global "them." Only once or twice has someone said, "We all are." And never has anyone shot back with, "I am."

Actively listening to people's responses to this simple but powerful question tells me whether this organization is made up of "workers" on autopilot—or "owners," individuals who see themselves as personally in charge of the organization's success and act accordingly in small and large ways. Owners, for instance, see litter in the bushes at work and instead of alerting the grounds keeper or ignoring it, actually stop, bend down and pick it up, throw it away and straighten up the area.

For Managers and Executives

There is one more aspect of the problem that I need to address before I offer a glimpse of the real solution. Those of us who currently have traditional hierarchical titles—such as senior director, supervisor, manager or vice president—intentionally or unintentionally keep people trapped in that old model by how we think and behave. In order to make room at the leadership table for everyone, we've got to let go of certain thoughts and actions. We've got to let go of:

- Viewing ourselves as organizational oracles and, along with it, our desire to know every answer and solve every problem single-handedly.
- Thinking of ourselves as the sole source of authority and power.
- Having tight control over absolutely everything.
- Holding on to erroneous perceptions and stereotypes about who can successfully lead at work.
- Fearing shared leadership with all others.
- Parenting, protecting, and rescuing others at work and the corresponding illusion that we "know best" and our way is always the best.
- Stroking our own egos.
- Stagnating in dysfunctional comfort.

There is a very important and often overlooked flip-side to leadership: followership. Leadership and followership are the yin and yang of business success. It is hard for some of us to accept the necessity to follow as well as lead because we're not used to seeing the value in the role of follower, especially as it relates to those who report to us on the organizational chart.

We must sense when to follow and when to lead. And we must value them both. In a practical sense, that means managers, directors, vice presidents, and presidents must sometimes get out of the way. A manager must tame her ego, open her ears, unlearn the fact that she has (or should have) all of the answers, practice humility, shut up more often, and pay attention to what everyone—even the temporary receptionist or the custodian—thinks.

We've got to get right with the idea that practicing followership is an important component of leadership and that sharing power, authority, and responsibility does not diminish us; in fact, it makes us stronger individually and collectively. Making space for everyone at the leadership table is a victory worth celebrating, not a loss to mourn. And we have got to understand that doing business as usual, being the way we've been for many years, is no longer a winning strategy.

All Hail the New Normal!

Because more and more of us are waking up to the fact that the same-old, same-old way of being and doing in business is underpowered to take us into the future, it just may be time for a revolution. Margaret Wheatley thinks so. In the foreword of the book, Authentic Conversations, Wheatley emphatically calls us to action: When people are bossed around, treated like robots and discarded casually, any sensible person disengages....it's time for a revolution...We simply cannot let this disintegration go any further.[5]

Ben & Roz Zander call out this same-old, same-old behavior by encouraging those of us who have leadership titles to recognize that our most important work is to "empower those we lead to realize their full potential and to become leaders themselves."[6]

Traditional ways of being together at work aren't working. That's the problem. But, perhaps as Tom Peters says, "the problem isn't the real problem. Our reaction to the problem is the problem."[7] All too often, our reactions to the growing awareness that the old, tired-but-familiar authoritarian model is on life support fall short of going far enough:

- We've tried to pretend or at least convince ourselves that it still works well.
- We've tweaked it a bit and worked harder to make it work.
- We've scratched our heads, wondered if there is something better, and concluded that the devil you know is better than the one that you don't and used that conclusion to stay stuck in dysfunctional comfortable habits.
- We've learned about new ways of being together that could make a difference but then allowed our inner cynics to take over. We tell ourselves that "it would never work here," because of _____ (fill in your preferred excuse).

None of these solutions are going to get us anywhere but more stuck, sort of like when your car gets stuck in mud or snow. When that happens, your first reaction is to push on the gas pedal. But that only makes the wheels spin harder which in turn digs them in deeper and you get more stuck. Take courage, though. There is a way out. And the work we do together in this book could be a refreshing adventure, infused with reality-based hope and complete with a roadmap to a different and better workplace experience.

The Solution:

Step Up To Coach Leadership

It's time to once and for all crack the code on the new way of doing business, to break away from who we've been in the past and break through to our new and better selves.

There are some of us who are already taking the risk of *doing* all that we can from where we are in our organizations; taking charge of our individual contribution at work; making a constructive difference; understanding how what we do each and every day relates to what others do; and how it moves us closer to our vision so that we can live our mission and meet our shared goals.

Tom Peters would applaud this reaction to the problem! If you are among these fearless pioneers, then bravo! You are engaged and well positioned to surge forward and keep the change in yourself and your organization alive. And that is where we all need to be headed, individually and collectively, if we are to break free from this vicious cycle in which we're stuck and replace it with a virtuous cycle.

Think of the many meanings of this word—*engage:*

- To attract
- To come together and interlock
- To be "in gear"
- To hold the attention of
- To induce to participate
- To pledge oneself or make a promise
- To be involved or to participate
- To begin and carry on with an enterprise

Uncanny, isn't it, how many of these are a match for what we need more of in our workplaces today?! Engagement demands that you assert yourself as a responsible leader; it requires that you demonstrate willingness and ability to do something more with your role, your goal, or your task. Let me say that again, willing to do more than expected!

What does engagement look like, practically?

If you are an engaged member of the cleaning team at work and your responsibility is to wax the floors, then find ways to be the best at that job. Look for ways to make the job more effective; save money through your ingenuity; take pride in how great the floors look when you've done your thing. Pat yourself on the back because great looking floors contribute to how satisfied customers generally are with your company.

And if you are an engaged temporary receptionist, you practice radical hospitality as you greet guests, bringing the full monty of your personality to the experience rather than simply doing the minimum, collecting a paycheck, and reminding yourself that you aren't even a "real" employee. And you take the risk of sharing your new ideas with others instead of holding back and assuming that no one would be interested in your view of things.

Or how extraordinary is it for an engaged housekeeper at the Ritz-Carlton hotel system to see herself as fully in charge of the overall experience of a guest and to take personal responsibility for making it right for a guest when something goes wrong? That's exactly what is happening now, and I applaud the Ritz-Carlton for allowing that housekeeper to independently make decisions, spend money to make it happen, and lead from her seat.[8]

The revolution to a workplace full of everyday leaders *is* possible. It can be done by you and by me. In fact, it already is! One person, one team, one department, one organization at a time.

Twelve years ago, I walked away from my corporate career path and founded my own leadership and business coaching enterprise, in part because I felt that there were few other options available to me to genuinely change the way that people work together. No matter how Pollyanna it may sound to some, I am dedicated to helping create different and better workplace experiences so that people don't need to exit the corporate world in order to be their best selves.

So, how do we get from here to there? What model or approach will offer each of us, regardless of position, the opportunity, confidence, and know how to engage as a responsible leader— to be different and to act differently?

Perhaps the answer lies in something so simple and so fundamental that we're almost unwilling or unable to see it for what it is. But what if there was an intentionally designed system for change based on communication that is results-oriented and stokes passion by removing obstacles to our success? That by its very nature helps create the environment where the everyday leader is able to take charge of his or her area and thrive as a result? That has as its end game full-throttle engagement?

Such a system exists, although it has been misunderstood and misused by many.

Ready? It's *coach leadership.*

And before anyone starts to protest, I'm here to set the record straight about the fierce potential that a universal leadership approach rooted in the coaching tradition has to change our work lives for good and forever. Think about it. Coaching is a long-standing, well-respected, even sacred tradition of one person helping another to be at their best. Influencers from all disciplines have used coaching as a powerful ally to exceed their goals.

So *forget what you think you know about coaching!* Don't allow that one bad experience with someone calling themselves a coach to color your opinion and wall you off from some of the most worthwhile learning of your life.

Set aside the following popular mis-conceptions that float around about coaching:
- Coaching is just an intervention when someone makes a mistake
- It's for "losers"
- Coaching is for sissies—it means that you're weak and ineffective
- It's a cool new label for the same-old, same-old disciplinary process of "writing people up"

- It's a twisted version of I'm okay-you're okay, therefore anything goes at work.

Instead, return with me to the roots of coaching. At its core, coaching is a directed conversation with oneself and with others that is aimed at helping, growing, and challenging. It is purposeful and skillful. It's about meaningful relationships. It's gutsy and results-driven because it requires everyone to be willing to tell the truth and find their own solutions—even to very difficult situations. It's edgy. It is the polar opposite of the old command and control model. One of the fundamental assumptions of the coaching tradition is that almost all people are capable, willing, creative, and bright adults. Coaching demands that everyone lead from their seat. The good news is that anyone can do it and it can be applied to all situations at work.

Allow me to be especially plainspoken for a moment. The coaching framework and its accompanying language offer a channel to reimagine, reinvent, reengineer, and then to revive our workplaces. Coaching is the energy conductor for raising the level of engagement and creating leaders in every seat. Coaching means that we believe in and then work toward bringing out the very best in ourselves and then others; this includes our boss, the boss's boss, our peers, our teammates, and those who may call us boss.

It is the essence of engagement!

And here's the neat part, you don't have to call yourself a coach or announce when you are coaching. In fact, you never need to use the verb "to coach." You just need to DO IT! Only then can you lead from your seat. Only then can you claim full engagement for yourself and for your organization.

Introducing: The Everyday Leadership Series

I firmly believe that coaching provides one of the best frameworks for activating and supporting the shared responsibility for changing who and how we are together in the workplace. This strong and unswerving belief is the inspiration and the spark of possibility that gave birth to this book series, Everyday Leadership.

The Solution

The Everyday Leadership series hinges on two common threads: (1) everyone in the organization is a leader, and (2) practicing universal coach leadership throughout the organization is the platform that allows that to happen and keeps it alive.

Everyday Leadership is intended to reinforce the notion that leadership is no longer reserved for the "C suites," the top floor, the "administration," "them," or those whose titles, positions, or ranks fall above some arbitrary threshold. In order for us to enjoy all dimensions of success, everyone in every job must be encouraged to view themselves as a leader. Every single one of us must lead from our seat.

The books in the Everyday Leadership series contain treasures for leaders at all levels—CEOs, the middle manager, and the front desk receptionist. As more and more people in an organization read the books in this series, a shared picture of the way forward and common language can be created. This enhances understanding and quickens the change cycle. We can make things better together faster!

The series is designed to build on itself. This initial volume on full-throttle engagement powered by coaching, Take the Lead, becomes the foundation upon which all other skills and aptitudes are built. No other work that I know of purports to represent coaching as the lynchpin to successful accountability, delegation, community, inclusion, and much more.

The Everyday Leadership Series supports the kaizen (Japanese, for improvement) approach to change, which is creating specific, incremental and usually modest changes until we evolve to the next level.

The series title also speaks to the simplicity of the books within the series, the practical nature of the program, and the fact that each and every day is filled with small, medium, and large opportunities for all to lead!

We need to collectively raise our level of awareness, redefine leading, recognize those powerful everyday moments of truth, those "leadership moments," and re-shape them to create individual, organizational, and community growth.

A Hero's Journey

So if you're up for it, welcome to the journey! Your organization, your community, your country, and your world need each of you to lead! How will you choose to experience this learning opportunity? For me, it isn't enough to think about our experience together as "reading (or listening to) another business book." Do that if you want to have an average experience. As an alternative, stop playing it safe and go ahead and set your expectations high. Allow for the possibility that this could be your wake-up call. Your "aha" moment. And be willing to participate in the learning as if that is the case.

This work is very personal. It requires personal commitment and personal responsibility. If you want to take a chance at having a great, life altering experience, then choose to view this as your own personal adventure. See yourself as the action hero/heroine in this book and view this work as a professional pilgrimage!

And I mean "action hero." Put yourself in the role of someone you think of as a hero. Think big. Superman. Luke Skywalker. Harry Potter. A neighbor leaving for military service in Afghanistan. A friend battling cancer. Your sister going through a painful divorce.

A hero to me is a regular person who leaves their routine behind because there is serious work to be done and they are called upon to do it. That's what I'm asking you to do. Take this book seriously. Leave your familiar world of work and take a leap from the known to the unknown, trusting that it will greatly benefit you and those around you. Find the courage to be different, to see things through a new lens, and to confront obstacles. This is the state of mind that has allowed me and many of my colleagues and clients to truly transform our work lives. I have never seen it fail.

The journey to full-throttle engagement I would like for you to travel through with me in this book is a hero's journey; the chapters are designed to mirror the path all heroes must take to vanquish the enemy, triumph over evil, and open the way for a new, better, and more fulfilled life for those who follow. The journey unfolds like this:

Step One: Preparation and Departure

Chapter 1 picks up where the back story leaves off and provides a much more detailed discussion of the changing nature of the global workplace and the role leadership plays in that today. It's important for us all to know where we've been together so that we can more fully understand the work ahead. This new awareness is the starting point for your professional pilgrimage. And it comes with a professional dare to intentionally leave behind the baggage from the past.

Step Two: The Adventure

Chapters 2 and 3 highlight the vital nature of engagement in today's workplace as a result of the seismic changes discussed in Chapter 1. It directly links high levels of engagement with coach leadership. It is here that you will gain a deep and rich understanding of what coach leadership is and what it is not. And what its true potential is in our workplaces. These chapters give us a sense that everything has got to change if we are to be successful together. It is a framework of possibility. It offers reality-based hope. And it reveals the road ahead.

Chapter 4 focuses on the role that intentionality plays in learning and discovery and growth -in change itself. It isn't easy to change, to become your best self. This is the point at which the action hero may still be thinking of turning back because the journey is too hard or too scary. This is also the point at which the hero fully commits to moving forward, even if it feels uncertain and risky. There is something telling him to keep moving.

Chapter 5 outlines the inner work that each of us must do in order to become a leader and commit wholeheartedly to full engagement. An imperative of this chapter is that we must first begin with ourselves—to coach ourselves by becoming very choiceful about what we think about and talk to ourselves about all day. Next, we must understand how to receive coaching messages from others around us and how to use that feedback in a healthy way. Only then, can we become a leader and help ourselves and others to be great.

Step Three: The Challenge and the Prize

Chapters 6 and 7 offer the skills and the know-how to coach and to lead from any seat. This is the point in any hero's journey when you become that new person. This is often a struggle. Here we confront old habits with new power and knowledge. It can feel unfamiliar and awkward. There is a series of tasks and dares that test your learning and your commitment. The goal here is to become a new you at work. If you want your organization to be fully engaged, then change yourself: mastering the skills of a coach is the challenge; proudly leading from your seat is the prize.

Step Four: The Return

Chapter 8 challenges us to take our new self and wisdom and weave it into the fabric of our everyday experiences at work. It offers suggestions for applying the learning to some all-too-typical situations in the workplace. It continues the work toward mastery. It helps us to sustain our new choices. And it reminds us that we are wise enough now to know when and how to ask for help!

Tallyho my friends! Give yourself the gift of time as you take in the knowledge and the power that comes with reading this book and living its message. Share a copy with a friend, colleague, your team, or your entire organization and journey together. Coaching frequently offers opportunities to take action or change something in order to allow yourself to move forward.

In that spirit, I have included at the end of each chapter, a "Coaching TO GO" section because I invite each of you to consider me as your success partner and coach throughout our journey together. Each contains calls to action to create change of some sort whether it be to provide an opportunity to apply the learning and make it stick with you; to assist you in finding your way and avoiding wrong turns; to move you toward your self-selected destination; and to avoid snap backs to old, worn out behaviors and to be true to the new you. Sometimes, the call to action takes the form of reflecting on tough issues; sometimes it's all about completing specific tasks that expand and deepen the learning or practicing a skill; and at other times, they feel more like a standing dare or personal challenge. What I ask you to do may take a few minutes, several hours or several days to complete. Stay with it. Connect your heart with your head. And do not censor yourself. Be exhaustive. Tell yourself the truth. If you do, you cannot get "it" wrong. Remember, also to take your time and embed this learning at a cellular level. Don't rush to be "done." My truth is that we never get this work completely done.

Together, let us consider the possibility that we are all leaders and the awesome potential that contains for unleashing greatness to carry us all forward. One of my most cherished quotes comes from Marianne Williamson's *A Return to Love*. This book has had such a meaningful impact on me personally and professionally. Whether you have read it many times or are reading it for the first time, I hope that it creates a spiritedness within you to challenge your own and your organization's definition of leadership so that you can move forward with courage, with conviction, with certitude that you are on the right path to real, lasting change.

> *"Who are you to play small? Our deepest fear is not that we are inadequate. Our deepest fear is that we are powerful beyond measure. It is our light, no our darkness that most frightens us. We ask ourselves, "Who am I to be brilliant, gorgeous, talented and fabulous? Actually, who are you not to be? You are a child of the universe. Your playing small does not serve you or your organization! There is nothing enlightened about shrinking so that other people won't feel insecure around you. We are all meant to shine as children do. We were born to manifest the glory of the universe that is within us. It's not just in some of us; it's in everyone. And as we let our own light shine, we unconsciously give other people permission to do the same. And as we are liberated from our own fear, our presence automatically liberates others."*
> **—Marianne Williamson**

Notes:

> "To lead people, walk beside them ... As for the best leaders, the people do not notice their existence. The next best, the people honor and praise. The next, the people fear; and the next, the people hate... When the best leader's work is done the people say, 'We did it ourselves!'"

—Lao-Tsu

From Status Quo to Status Go!

A Context Ripe for Change

"There's something happening here. What it is ain't exactly clear."
—Buffalo Springfield

I remember the first time that I used the Buffalo Springfield quote above with a large live audience. I wanted to ignite some lively dialogue about the context within which we as leaders work and the changing nature of leadership. It popped into my mind during my preparation in one of those amazing "aha" moments and I was, I admit, pretty confident that it would be a clever introduction to this provocative topic. I felt even more confident as I walked into the expansive ballroom for my speaking engagement and actually heard the words being sung by Buffalo Springfield over the sound system during registration. I chuckled to myself as it hit me that those hosting this leadership conference had also thought it to be perfectly aligned with the theme of quantum change in business.

As I began my presentation, I caught more than a few puzzled looks in the audience, particularly from my younger colleagues. Finally, a brave soul raised her hand and said, "Exactly who is Buffalo Springfield?" The baby boomers in the audience laughed and the Generation X and

Millennials in attendance all shook their head in approval of the question and the need for clarification. So much for clever ideas.

For those of you who don't recognize this lyric or haven't yet Googled it, Buffalo Springfield was a short-lived but influential folk rock group in the sixties.[9] This line is from what many consider to be their most famous song "For What It's Worth, " and the song has come to symbolize the worldwide turbulence and confrontational feelings arising from events during that time period: unrest, need for something different, recognizing that what had come before wasn't going to be able to take that generation into the future.

I believe we as business leaders are facing challenges and opportunities of the same magnitude as the societal changes of the 1960s. As I pointed out in the End Game section, we all get that there really is something "happenin'" in business—the same unrest, the need for something different.

An informal survey of business executives indicates that many believe that change is a business constant and that it will remain so for at least the next two decades. In addition, most believe that the rate at which change occurs will continue to accelerate. An interesting bit of information that highlights how rapidly our world is changing is this: half of all change in recorded time has happened only since 1940!

Like those business executives, I believe that we are riding powerful, perhaps unprecedented currents of change in business—currents that are leading us towards the radical restructuring of the way we work that I call "everyday leadership." It's a workplace cultural revolution. My own research suggests that this shift has been happening incrementally for three or more decades. And in much the same way as the Allegheny and the Monongahela Rivers join to form that mighty force of nature, the Ohio River, in Pittsburgh, Pennsylvania (my home state), a number of powerful business forces are converging to make conditions ripe for the dramatic shift we need to create the new kind of business leader, the everyday kind that leads from his or her seat. In other words, we have reached what Malcolm Gladwell calls a "tipping point," a moment of critical mass, the threshold, the boiling point when the momentum for change becomes unstoppable.[10]

A new idea is first condemned as ridiculous and then dismissed as trivial, until finally it becomes what everybody knows.

—William James

From Industrial to Conceptual

A broad review of business writing and research over the past twenty years suggests that there are five big, hairy forces of change that have brought us to this tipping point and continue to urge and propel us forward. From my vantage point, these five primary drivers of change in business are:

1. Technology
2. Demographics (the dynamic balance of populations)
3. Government
4. Economy
5. Environment

Individually, each of these is tremendously powerful. In combination with one another, they become even more potent change agents. Allow me to share a personal story with you to highlight both the interactive nature of these forces and just how active and influential these forces are in our everyday lives.

One of my everyday heroes was my dad. He died at the age of ninety-four and was blessed with a sharp mind and a quick wit until the very end of his life. Shortly before his ninetieth birthday, he needed to have the aortic valve in his heart replaced. He consulted a surgeon in his hometown in Western Pennsylvania and they agreed that my dad would undergo surgery to remove the leaky valve and replace it with a bovine valve. (As an aside, the new valve came with a fifteen-year "warranty." When the surgeon looked my father in the eye and said, "This new valve will function for fifteen years," my Dad looked back and without missing a beat asked, "What will we do then?" My dad's framework of positivity is one of the reasons he is long lived!)

My father's surgery went well. Following the operation, the surgical team did a diagnostic test to be sure that the new valve and my father's heart were functioning properly. Now one would think that the physicians who reviewed his diagnostic test and prepared the report would have been in the same hospital. They weren't. They weren't even both located in Pittsburgh. In fact, the doctor who reviewed all the information was in India! Why was a physician in India handling this part of my dad's care? Because it was cheaper than using a doctor in the hospital and of equal quality.

Let's step back and think of how four of the five forces of change in business play a role in my dad's case:

Technology allowed the Indian physician to see the results of the diagnostic test in real time.

Ninety-year-olds in the U.S. are having their heart valves replaced. Many of us are living longer, healthier lives. The Indian professional labor force continues to grow and more and more professional services around the world are now being performed by Indian professionals. Both of these are evidence of demographic shifts.

Licensure, safety, and quality standards must be met in healthcare and, in this case, it required the synergistic cooperation of several governments.

The hospital's interest to be as cost effective as possible was, most likely, the primary motivation behind the decision to use an Indian physician. Economic considerations changed the old (traditional) way of doing business at this hospital.

The convergence of these forces has given rise to what I hinted at throughout the back story, what I call the "itch for occupational adventure." Because the U.S. workforce is no longer satisfied with their current experience, and because even in uncertain economic times they want something different, something more, I think we can now say that we're finally casting off the Industrial Age way of thinking and acting. We're no longer factory workers who need to be watched and monitored, obeying all commands from the top in order to get a paycheck. No longer is a layer of managers and supervisors necessary to make sure that people are working and doing the work "right."

Those of us who watch cultural trends know that historians and thought leaders have a long tradition of naming the "age" that characterizes the general population during a specified period of time. Many thought leaders believe that the changes we are experiencing right now are so profound as to move us, rather quickly and abruptly, into a different "age."

When the U. S. was founded, the people lived in what is called the Agricultural Age. With the advent of machines to do the work humans once did, the Industrial Age was born. With the rise of the computer, we slowly moved into the Information Age, where the products produced are knowledge-based rather than manufactured. The movement is clear: from no collar to blue collar to white collar work. It's the inevitable flow of history. As automation driven by technology transformed farming, and as the world grew flatter and many manufacturing jobs moved to other parts of the world, the same pattern emerged for knowledge work: automated or offshored. What's next?

Economists tell us that we are in the later stages of the Information Age, and this transitional time is sometimes called the "Experience Age" because we in the U.S. want to buy more and more experiences. A meal in the best restaurant in town isn't just about fueling our bodies. It's about the lighting, the presentation, the service, the music, the furniture, and artwork. Think about a trip to Disneyworld—it's the experience we're after. And we are willing to pay a lot for that experience.

Many thought leaders believe that the next economic time will be called the Conceptual Age or the Age of Inspiration. Daniel Pink, Tom Peters, and others tell us that we have moved through an economy built on people's backs to an economy built on people's logic to what is emerging today: an economy of high tech and high touch that flows from emotional and intuitive intelligence. Sometimes, shift happens!

From the Agriculture Age to Conceptual Age

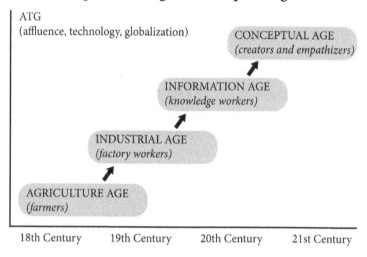

ATG
(affluence, technology, globalization)

CONCEPTUAL AGE
(creators and empathizers)

INFORMATION AGE
(knowledge workers)

INDUSTRIAL AGE
(factory workers)

AGRICULTURE AGE
(farmers)

18th Century   19th Century   20th Century   21st Century

*"If you don't like change, you're going to
like irrelevance a whole lot less."*
—General Shinsiki

The idea behind the "Conceptual Age" is punctuated by universal workplace education and the freedom to act. It promotes the kind of business structure that allows for a collaborative, classless approach—the kind that allows for all members of an organizational community to lead from their seat.

Because organizational structure is changing, who we are being called forth to *be* at work is also changing, dramatically for many of us! New definitions of who we are and what we are here for are emerging. As we described earlier, a new and different set of expectations within the workforce is making a heavy contribution to this shift. Generational differences in expectation, for example, are providing significant traction and momentum for this transformation. Even Baby Boomers (those of us roughly between the ages of forty-seven and sixty-three) are increasingly looking for greater measures of freedom at work as well. As this influential "age wave" changes, so do the institutions that they lead. This transformation is captured well in the Center for Creative

Leadership's (CCL) current leadership priorities. As I interpret the CCL research findings, they encourage us to grow the following attributes in ourselves and others to meet the new challenges and opportunities of the coming age:

- Flexibility
- Collaboration
- Cross pollination (easily and willingly sharing our knowledge, information, insight, and solutions broadly within our organization for the overall good of that very same organization; it is the opposite of building organizational silos)
- Connected or collective leadership (sharing power and authority broadly and seeing that as a victory rather than a loss)

Connectivity. Collective leadership. Conceptual versus Industrial. These words and the ideas they convey all point to something that is no longer same-old, same-old but something that *is* refreshing, the idea that we're all in this together, that it is up to each of us to make the organization, the business, the team, the group—name it what you will—a success.

What's interesting to me is that fueling this transformation is an impending leadership "vacuum." Many current organizational leaders who grew up with a command-and-control model will be of an age to either retire or "refire" (go on to other pursuits). Consider this: 40 percent of family owned businesses in the U.S. will change top leadership within the next five years! Given, that 90 percent of American companies are family-owned in whole or in part, this is an unprecedented shift in power. What does this mean? Fresh faces will abound, carrying with them a different set of expectations and perspectives. And sparks of possibility will be created. Will we try to cling to our familiar, maladaptive Industrial Age ways? Or will we play big and move toward a new way of leading from every seat? I'm betting on the latter.

Extraordinary thought leaders are offering up a blue print for the leadership model of the Conceptual Age. One of them is Daniel Pink. I offered his chart above from his breakthrough book, *A Whole New Mind*. There he makes a compelling case that because of the overpowering forces of change that we have discussed, we are indeed entering a new business world built on invention, empathy, and big-picture thinking.

But here's the kicker: according to Pink, in order to successfully make the jump into this new space, we must surrender our longstanding over-reliance on our left brains and *lead with our right brains!*

This is huge.

Our right brains are the centers of our emotions. It's the part of our brain that is normally attributed to artists because it's the part of our brain that is used when our minds are in creative-process mode. It allows for big-picture thinking, helps us to connect dots, and builds and maintains lasting, robust relationships. Think about that for a minute. Instead of logic, creativity matters more. Instead of rational thinking, feelings and relationships matter more in the future.[11]

In the Conceptual Age, connecting with one another in fresh ways will be the new pathway to success. The high-tech, high-touch workplace of the future means that we must not only connect with our emotional and intuitive intelligence, but we must lead from this new place. Christopher Hegarty agrees. In the *7 Secrets of Exceptional Leadership*, he asserts that, in the future, 80 – 85 percent of the factors leading to success will arise from these two intelligences with the remaining 15 – 20 percent from the logic.[12] In other words, for those of us who are still trapped in the old "command and control" model, we must do a "cerebral hokey pokey," putting our whole brains into our work and our relationships. Maybe, as the song says, this really is "what it's all about!"

I recently came across a brilliant example of the shift to right-brain creative thinking that is occurring. Alexis Wary is the nine-year-old daughter of Andrea Wary, one of my healthcare colleagues in Pennsylvania. When discussing the changing nature of leadership in early 2010, my colleague shared Alexis' creation (then seven), called "fashion math." This future right-brain leader created this framework to put arithmetic problems in a context that felt "right" to her and to facilitate her understanding and learning. One of her fashion-math equations is pictured below. Very clever!

For me, it is a perfect example of what Pink is talking about when he says we're quickly moving into the Conceptual Age. I'm betting that Alexis will do well leading from her seat!

Integrated leadership thinking, with the right-brain dominant, is gaining traction and moving us forward toward a healthier and more engaged organizational culture. This new level of awareness and framework for action is allowing many of us to turn an important corner. We no longer have to settle at getting better and better at a model that is "wronger" and "wronger."

This road that we are traveling together is taking us closer and closer to living in a more fully engaged workplace, characterized by:

- Intentional creation of leaders in all seats
- A framework of possibility
- Ownership of the entire organization's success—people acting as adult, capable organizational citizens
- Alignment of our daily work activities with the organization's vision, mission, values, and direction as well as with one another
- Passion for both learning *and* unlearning
- High quality relationships
- Habit of unbridled celebration

These are the characteristics of *full-throttle engagement*, and they will become our everyday experience as more of us pull our seats up to that leadership table. If we want this badly enough, believe that it is possible, and stay focused on doing our part, it won't be too long before people like Martha the store clerk become the rule rather than the exception. We'll discuss each of these in more detail in the next chapter.

Coaching TO GO

Still hungry for more learning? Want to make the learning stickier? Try these on for size to expand your perspective and turn knowledge into power! Stoke the fire. Keep the learning alive. Do the maximum, rather than the minimum!

1. **Watch the video**—Have you seen the "Did you know?" 3.0 video? It deals with the global impact of several of the big hairy forces for change that we discussed. It is well done and almost always ignites a lively conversation.

2. **What a difference a century makes!**—If you want to take a look at just how far we have come in the last one-hundred years, visit our website and check out some mind boggling fast facts from 1908.

3. **Lending library**—Does your organization have a lending library (books, electronic downloads, CDs)? If not, go on a crusade and get one started. It is a terrific way to stimulate new thinking, get conversations rolling and challenge the status quo.

4. **Must haves for your professional library**—If you want to make yourself smarter about the seismic changes happening, add any/all of these best sellers for a rich read. Better yet, create a leadership learning circle and read them with a group of your colleagues and share your reactions.

   - *The World Is Flat* by Thomas L. Friedman
   - *Hot, Flat and Crowded* by Thomas L. Friedman
   - *Re-imagine* by Tom Peters
   - *A Whole New Mind* by Daniel Pink
   - *The Art of Possibility* by Benjamin & Rosamund Zander

5. **Pay attention to generational trends** (demographics)—Visit the experts at www.gentrends.com to learn more.

6. **Step back in time and take another listen (or a first time listen) to Buffalo Springfield's legendary song, "For What it is Worth."**

Notes:

2 Full-Throttle Engagement:

Redefining Our Way of Work

I've never had control and I never wanted it. If you create an
environment where people truly participate, you don't need control.
—Herb Kelleher, Founder & Executive Chairman of
the Board of Southwest Airlines

The forces brewing that will culminate in acceptance of the Conceptual Age are nothing short of a "perfect storm." They signal the emergence of that something "new" in the workplace we've all hungered for but perhaps were too afraid to put words to.

Take heart. The stage is set. Now, we collectively need to, first, recognize this as an opportunity whose time has arrived; second, resist that strong temptation to hold onto traditional ways of working together than really aren't that successful anymore; and, third, take a chance and start *acting* differently toward one another and our work.

Imagine this—you look forward to going to work most days. You're tuned in, tapped in, and turned on while you're there. You are invested and involved. Time flies by for you. You actually get "your work" done, whatever that is for you. And you get it done during work hours instead of playing a never ending game of catch-up in the evenings or worrying and feeling guilty over the weekend. You feel listened to, even appreciated and valued most days. You are crystal clear about how what you do each day matters to your clients or your customers (I didn't say "the company's clients" or "customers" on purpose here). Yes, what you do makes a difference. You can easily connect the dots between your work and the organization's success.

Now picture this—your colleagues and teammates are doing the same! You and your work mates have mutually respectful relationships that are based on a sense of community. Most people there act as though "we are all in this together," helping each other and pushing each other to greatness is a widespread practice.

There's definitely "something happenin' here," but it is now very clear to you what it is. Your organization is changing. Your boss asks your opinion about challenges and expects your help in finding solutions. There's widespread involvement in all aspects of work. Rarely does someone say, "that's not in my job description." People own their mistakes and are willing to tell the truth instead of trying to constantly cover their rear. Everyone, it seems, holds an unswerving focus on WOWing the customer. In fact, all take pride in doing so.

In the new world of business, problems and challenges exist. This isn't a utopia. But with those problems comes solutions and opportunities—solutions that didn't come from the top but from the people actually doing the doing. The pace of work is relentlessly fast, but the working environment is such that everyone thrives on the challenges that presents. The organization is more nimble and healthier because, embedded in the organization as a *core belief*, is the notion that every employee is a leader, leading from his or her seat. Everyone acts differently because of that belief. Every employee is **engaged**, making progress on their work activities with total commitment.

No, we didn't just step through the looking glass. This isn't some unattainable Wonderland and you are not Alice! This is what full-throttle engagement looks like and feels like at work. And we can co-create it together *by individually daring to* **Take The Lead!**

It is possible. It's already happening in small ways and large in departments, divisions, and entire organizations around the world. More companies are thriving, even in difficult economic times, because of their level of employee engagement. And it can happen in your workplace as well. As we become more purposeful in contributing to its creation in our workplace, it will eventually become our reality.

Engagement Equals Success

There is growing evidence that engagement and business success are directly linked. The more engaged we all are at work, the more profitable and successful our entire organization is. In their book, *The Elements of Great Managing*, Rodd Wagner and James K. Harter conclude that "the evidence is clear that the creation and maintenance of high employee engagement, as one of the few determinants of profitability largely within a company's control, is one of the most crucial imperatives of any successful organization."[13]

Wagner and Harter, who work for the Gallop polling service, also offered the following fast facts linking engagement and success:

- Workgroups whose engagement level puts them in the bottom quartile of the Gallup database average 62 percent more accidents.
- Engaged employees average 27 percent less absenteeism.
- Having higher levels of team engagement equates to 12 percent higher customer service scores than those in the bottom tier.
- Teams in the top engaged quartile are three times more likely to succeed as those in the bottom quartile, averaging 18 percent higher productivity and 12 percent higher profitability.
- In publicly traded companies, engaged organizations outperformed the earnings per share of their competitors by 18 percent and over time progressed at a faster rate than their industry peers.

If your eyes just glazed and you're mumbling *enough already with the statistics*, I ask you to take another look at how profound and even shocking some of these numbers really are. I want you to realize what's at stake here. I want you to understand deeply that what we are talking about is not just another fad or flashy program. People who are more engaged work more effectively, and that impacts everyone's bottom line. An engaged workforce co-creates a unique kind of energy together that is so magnetic that the organization becomes the kind of place where people say "I'm proud to work here; I'm excited about coming to work; I want to leave a legacy of contribution."

The following chart captures the ongoing evolution of our way of life at work from the traditional "command and control" model to full-throttle engagement. As you review the primary characteristics of each, ask and answer the following questions:

Q. Which of these approaches best describes my organization today?

Q. Which best describes my thoughts and behaviors at work?

Q. Which of these approaches feels better to me? Why?

Q. Which would allow me to grow into my best self?

Q. What am I prepared to do today to be more fully engaged at work?

Traditional versus Engaged Organization

Traditional Organizational Characteristics	Engaged Organizational Characteristics
Command and control culture	Leaders coach and nurture
Status quo	Culturally vibrant
Top are thinkers & deciders, bottom are doers	Everyone is a thinker & decider. Everyone has power
Numbers and quotas are of primary value	Quality is the primary value
Information flows primarily downward; only good news flows up	Information moves in all directions: listening, learning and questioning are everywhere
Conflict is viewed as bad and readily dismissed	Conflict is seen as a potential avenue for improvement and innovation
Extrinsic motivators dominate: pay, benefits, status symbols	Intrinsic motivators are important: involvement, ownership, acknowledgement and respect
Short-term planning and payoff	Long-term vision and payoff
Internal independence and competition	Horizontal teamwork and cooperation
Isolated layers and structures	Integrated vertical teams
Midlevel grid specialists control and enforce.	Midlevel leaders share expertise and vision with strong internal customer orientation
Employee evaluation based on punitive assumptions and tools	Positive orientation towards people with emphasis on quality and development—life-long learning
Machine analogy (impersonal)	
Rigid rules, policies and programs	
Customer (internal and external) is seen as a passive recipient	Living organism/ system analogy
	"Loose anchors": outcome criteria, benchmarks, and guidelines
	Customer seen as an ally, partner and active participant

So, where do you stand when it comes to your level of engagement?

1. Being **engaged** is our individual responsibility and our choice. It means that you show up each day at work with a passion for what you do and a profound connection to the vision, mission, values, and direction of your organization. You choose to donate "surplus energy" at work. To DuPont manager, Richard Knowles, that means bringing energy, enthusiasm, and a hunger for peak performance beyond the minimum required to keep a *j-o-b. Is this you?*

    For my colleagues who are already engaged at work, this book will affirm your approach, provide you with specific suggestions for maintaining your level of engagement, and help you to become more sophisticated in all of your interactions so that your leadership will model the way for others. How good can you stand it?

    Dominique, the team leader of the copy center at my local office supply store, is a stellar example of someone who practices full-throttle engagement! She finds creative solutions; peppers her conversations with humor and affection that delight the customers; is constructive; asks great questions; and treats her colleagues as though they were special, smart, capable, and precious to her. Her favorite phrase is, "That was easy!"

2. Are you currently choosing **not to be engaged?** Those who aren't engaged are putting in time rather than energy and passion. We've all heard the clever descriptions of this type of coworker: "dead-worker walking" or "retired while on active duty." Who wants to be that? More to the point—who wants to work with someone like that? These are the employees who are indifferent and can be cynical and dispirited. Checked out. My experience is that disengaged colleagues were once hopeful and constructive. But they've been hurt, disappointed, or have given up or given in to negativity. *Is this you?*

    The problem with not choosing to be engaged is that you can easily find yourself trapped here in a downward spiral; I have never seen anything constructive come from remaining aloof and uncaring at work. It is *not enough* to show up each day! For those who are not engaged today, this book offers a practical way up and forward for you. Don't give up on yourself and your organization and stop settling. Take a risk here, do the work, and allow yourself to believe that you are in charge of you and that something better is possible.

I remember a discussion I had with Roy, a security guard at a corporate center, about the toxic nature of gossiping about one's colleagues. He looked at me with a blank expression on his face and said, "What would we talk about if we didn't gossip...seriously what else is there to talk about?" Now that's an example of someone stuck in old, unproductive habits of thought!

3. Those of us who are **actively disengaged** aren't simply unhappy or dissatisfied, we are often acting out our negative feelings. Unfortunately for everyone, many times that acting out includes undermining what engaged workers are accomplishing. Gallup estimates that the lower productivity levels of the actively disengaged costs the U.S. economy $300 billion annually! *Is this you?*

The simple fact that you can acknowledge that this pattern matches your current choices and that you are reading/listening to this book is cause for optimism. This work will be challenging. You must look in the mirror, peel back the cynicism and defensiveness, and tell yourself the unvarnished truth about your habits and how destructive they can be for you personally and for your organization. And you've really, really got to want to act differently badly enough to get out of your own way!

I recently encountered someone who was spreading rumors and actively undermining a coworker to get even with her for something that happened a long time ago. This person was willing to sacrifice the well-being of their organization in favor of pursuing this vendetta (and actually said so).

Signs of Engagement

Organizations that demonstrate high levels of engagement share seven important characteristics. And they're not simply paid lip service;

they actually believe in them, live them through everyday action, and do regular self- assessments to stay on track. I call them the Signs of Engagement. The surprising truth is that all of these are simple. Deceptively so. Just because they are simple does not mean that they are easy for us to do day in and day out. For many of us, they do not reflect our current habits at work. That means that if you want to experience more engagement at work, you've got to be willing to change—change your thinking, your feelings, and your behavior.

How many of these do you practice regularly?

Sign #1—Everyone is expected to lead from their seat. In the acting profession, it is often said that "there are no small parts, only small actors." The same is true for successful organizations. There are NO small positions. (Return to the Backstory for specific examples of what this looks and feels like.) With the expectation that everyone leads comes the learning, tools, support, and freedom needed to make it so. Those of us who have a title such as manager or president view this sharing of power with others as a victory, not a loss or threat.

At a forward thinking healthcare system in Western Pennsylvania, the President/CEO regularly sends the clear message that leadership is everyone's job. There was a memorable moment at a town hall during which he forcefully said (paraphrasing) that no one would ever be "in trouble" for disagreeing with him or anyone else in public or private. Such conversations need to be respectful but they are welcome. In fact, he went on to say that team members should be more concerned if they are holding back an opinion, insight, or solution that could move the organization ahead to a more favorable position! And he gave everyone permission to make an appointment to come to his office and talk with him if they have a different experience anywhere in the system. Now that's putting in on the line. That's bold.

Sign #2—Individually and collectively, we work in a framework of possibility and positivism and have a constructive approach to problem resolution. Only from here can we tap into the creativity and innovation that will allow us to enjoy new lives of success.

Sign #3—Every person accepts responsibility for the overall success of the ENTIRE organization in addition to taking responsibility for completing his/her individual responsibilities with integrity, goodwill, accuracy, thoroughness, and dedication to the recipient of the organization's services/products (our customers).

At a recent stay at a Hilton property in Texas, I had a firsthand experience of this level of personal accountability for an everyday leader named Joachim. He took an OW customer experience and turned it into WOW. The previous night there was a group of guests partying on my floor until 3:30AM. I did not get the night's sleep that I wanted and needed to be at my best the next morning. Joachim was the customer service representative at the front desk when I showed up to tell my story. I asked for the manager (yes, my bad! I should have believed that Joachim could work with me to make it right). Joachim asked me to tell him my problem and assured me that he could help. And he was absolutely true to his word. After hearing my story, the first thing that he said was how sorry he was that I had missed out on a good night's sleep. Then he said it was his goal to make up for my disappointment. He immediately owned the situation. And he addressed my situation with creativity and fairness: I did not pay for that night's stay AND I received additional "points" to be redeemed in the future! Needless to say that I never needed to talk to the manager. Way to go, Joachim: an everyday leader, leading from his seat.

Sign #4—Everyone understands and is *personally aligned* with the vision, mission, values, and direction of the organization. That means that it is our responsibility to choose to be lined up, in sync with, and focused on these core beliefs. Equally important is the need to be in sync with our colleagues. We position ourselves to support others at work, to understand how things come together to create the best possible outcome for our customer. We challenge current barriers to lining up with one another, including stale policies, outdated physical spaces, dysfunctional customs and habits, even some of our thoughts and the language that we routinely use. This work is often called "silo busting." Working in silos is an "anti-collaboration" way of being together at work in which we isolate ourselves from other departments or divisions and adopt an us/them mentality. Think the corporate office versus actual sites of service (stores, clinics, branch offices). Instead, think Three Musketeers—all for one and one for all.

Sign #5—Everyone accepts the leadership dare of fostering high-quality relationships at work! Engagement brings with it an absolute obligation to be in "right relationship" with all others in the organization. We are all in the business of people growing. Sometimes, it's hard at first to understand that I have a responsibility for helping someone to grow who is above me on the organizational chart. And, no, we don't need to be drinking or shopping buddies with everyone. But we all must practice civility, respect, and consideration and re-dedicate ourselves to truth telling and healthy, meaningful conflict. In a national survey, *Gallup Management Journal* found that the quality of workplace relationships were substantially different for engaged and actively disengaged employees. Engaged employees are more likely to say that their organization encourages close friendships at work, that their boss sets them up for success and that colleagues complement their strengths.

Sign #6—Everyone shares a passion for both learning and un-learning and a *strong* bias toward really effective communication. That means that we've got to be willing to let go of old ways of thinking; we have to develop a healthy distrust of our own perceptions and assume that we only have a part of the picture; we must tell and listen to stories that connect us all together; and we must be okay with not knowing it all.

Rule #7—Everyone makes the time for unbridled celebration. We recognize individual and collective success; we salute bold failures and we learn from our mistakes. We slow down to speed up!

If you're saying to yourself right about now, "well, duh . . . who wouldn't want work to be this way!" you aren't alone. In my experience, most people genuinely want to be more engaged and want to work in organizations in which most people are more engaged as well. If that's true, then what keeps getting in our way?

More and more organizations are responding to the changing nature of work and reaching new levels of engagement. One obvious give away of such change is the reimagining or complete removal of titles of any type. Removing or intentionally changing titles is a small but meaningful initial step to encouraging leadership from every single seat. Discontinuing the use of titles that support the old notion that some are leaders and some are not is the cure for what I fondly call the "pecking order syndrome."

Affiniscape is one such business that has chosen to rethink their use of titles to identify a person's talent or area of expertise. James, a member of the Affiniscape team, shares his title-less business card that simply reads "Sales."

Tom's Shoes is also removing hierarchical barriers and encouraging a workplace full of leaders. As a result, owner and founder, and president Blake Mycoskie identifies himself as "chief shoe giver," instead of President or CEO.

If these changes seem subtle to you, you're right. But I always say "big doors swing on small hinges." Change and transformation often show up first as incremental but intentional shifts. Subtle change often is significant change! Don't dismiss it. It also gives you the opportunity to begin to create change immediately. It doesn't have to be a home run. It just needs to be change.

Success Equation

From my vantage point, what derails us from being more fully engaged is that we don't know *how* to get there. We're missing the actions that will deliver more engagement. We get stuck trying to figure out what to do differently.

Fortunately, the answer is hidden in plain sight. We simply need to adjust our lens to be able to see it. One framework for seeing things differently that has been beneficial to me and many of my clients is what I call my "success equation." It's been written about by Neale Donald Walsch, Robert Allen, and Mark Victor Hansen and probably many others.[15] My success equation is:

BE—DO—HAVE

It's actually quite an ingenious equation that works in a remarkably simple way. In order to set this success equation in motion is to ask yourself what you (or we) want to *have* at work. Then, ask yourself who you would *be* if you had that. Finally, ask yourself what would you be *doing* if you were that person?

In the Backstory, I introduced the idea of what you need to *be*: someone who leads from his or her seat, and who takes responsibility for the entire organization, regardless of title, position, salary level, or parking space location. In this chapter, I have given you an in-depth look at what you *have* when you are a successful coach leader—full-throttle engagement. "Full-throttle" means that you're going all out. It comes from car-talk, when the gas line is fully open. No stops. No barriers. If we can agree that having full-throttle engagement is a win for everyone in the workplace and being a leader regardless of your position is the key to full engagement, then we have two of the three parts of the equation:

BE A LEADER From Your Seat → HAVE FULL ENGAGEMENT

The third element in the success equation, the "doing" part, is really pivotal. It is vital to name what you want to be so that you know what you want to have. The middle part can either be a vast chasm filled with "to do" lists not checked off, goals set but not met, frustrated dreams and commitments; or it can be a superhighway of activity, where individuals have action plans and know how to get them done. In other words, the "doing" part is the essential middle because without it the other two parts simply remain as potential. Nothing moves forward without taking action, without doing something different.

Fortunately, there is a "doing" part, a proven system that includes the mindset and the skill set to ennoble each of us to leadership and enable widespread engagement. I named it as the solution in the Backstory: coach leadership. It is the systematic way to achieving widespread engagement *because* it positions everyone to lead in such a way that those around them feel helped, capable, and elevated.

I believe that the success equation that will allow us to transform our workplaces and complete the jump from the old to the new is:

BE A LEADER FROM YOUR SEAT

DO COACH WITH EVERYONE AROUND YOU

HAVE FULL-THROTTLE ENGAGEMENT

It allows for the creativity and connectedness called for in the Conceptual Age, but it is not some "airy-fairy" idea that sounds good on paper but doesn't work in the real world. It has proven itself to work over and over in the companies that have adopted it. I personally have found that it turbo charges my clients and their organizations into high levels of production; but more importantly, the everyday leaders who people those organizations feel like they work with purpose, passion, and the conviction that they matter.

Wouldn't you like to have that for yourself and your organization?

Notes:

3 Framework of Possibility:

The Coach Leader Approach To Full-Throttle Engagement

*Coaching is about inspiring, empowering, enabling people
to live deeply in the future, while acting boldly in the present.*
—Robert Hargrove

I can almost hear the buzz in your minds—coaching? Really? How can that possibly help an entire organization become more engaged, more "tuned in, tapped in…" and whatever else that third thing was that you were talking about earlier on in chapter2? (That would be "turned on"—the best one right?!)

To answer your question, let's think about an everyday workplace situation. Out of the blue, your boss tells you to jump in and put out an organizational "fire" and you immediately feel unprepared, ill equipped, overwhelmed, and don't know who to turn to or what resources are available. You feel a little bit like the comedian, Lily Tomlin, when she said, "We're all in this alone."

Or what about this: you've got lots of pretty good ideas, you see ways that things can be both better and different, and yet you feel as though you're invisible. No one listens and you continue to be told to do things in a way that makes less and less sense and no longer gets the job done well.

The list of "or, or, or" could go on and on, but this is why coach leadership works. With this system, a very different "or" list emerges. Instead of feeling like you don't know anything or can't do anything right, you can safely ask: "I don't know, can you help me figure it out?" or "I'm not sure but this is what I think would work," or "Hey, I may have a better way of doing this task, would you like to hear about it," or "What do you think we should do? You're the real expert here." (I'll take this latter list of "or, or, or" anytime—what about you?)

To put it at a thirty-thousand foot view, coaching is all about positive change, growth, and discovery—all big concepts—but the reality is that coaching gets you all those really neat things because in essence coaching is a directed conversation that happens all the time, every day, and has purpose and structure. Conversation is the most ancient and easiest way to cultivate the conditions for change. Coaching is thoughtful conversation purposefully focused on bringing out the best in oneself and in others to achieve meaningful goals. When it's done right, the people involved in the conversation feel listened to, satisfied, and acknowledged; and the benefit to the organization is that everyday leaders who use coaching wow each other and their customers. Every person. Every interaction. Every time.

It creates fully-engaged individuals in an organization because it is about each person taking ownership of their work, their relationships, and the overall success of the joint. When each person participates actively as a coach leader, they become the architect of the answer, the solution, the innovation. If you ever had to read Henry David Thoreau's Walden Pond in high school or college, you'll remember that Thoreau lived for two years, two months, and two days in a cabin he built by Walden Pond in Massachusetts. He wanted to find out "why he lived and what he lived for," and it is a classic of American literature because it expresses a fundamental aspect of American individualism, also sometimes called the rugged individual: in order for a group to be strong, each individual member of that group must be strong and know what he or she is all about. Coaching strengthens the individual and, so by extension, the group. As such, it is framed as an opportunity. That's what makes universal coach leadership so "sticky," and why it, more often than not, brings with it sustainable change and growth, why it becomes the "doing" part of full-throttle engagement.

Universal Coach Leadership 101

For me, the emerging Conceptual Age or what has sometimes been called the Age of Inspiration, is indeed, the Age of the Coach Leader. I think you get by now that I don't define leadership by what seat you occupy, by your position, or by your title. Leading is something that a person does, and for an organization to truly succeed, to soar, we must increasingly cultivate a leadership mindset in absolutely everyone! There is absolutely no doubt in my mind that full-throttle engagement leads directly to renewed and even expanded success across industries and disciplines.

So the Conceptual Age is all about creating leaders in every seat within an organization to achieve peak performance and universal coach leadership (yes, that means everyone practices it at all times). It is the framework of possibility, complete with a different language, to make that happen.

Virtually all of us have heard the term "coaching" and have an understanding of the role that a coach can play in achieving individual or team success. In fact, the coaching framework was borrowed by the business community from other disciplines. Where have most of us heard of coaching? Sports, of course. Think for a moment about legendary baseball or football players, the best in the world at their job. Do you think that each of them has a coach? Yes, several in fact. Does that make those players "losers"? Of course not! Coaches have a different perspective than players do. Coaches can see things that the player may miss on his own; can ask provocative questions; can challenge same-old, same-old thinking and behaving; can positively challenge an athlete to ask more of himself. Coaches offer options to take advantage of opportunities or move around obstacles quickly and easily and can help him to be at his very best. Follow any sport and you'll always hear the players, the commentators, even the fans talk about how a good coach can make even the best become better.

Another discipline in which the coaching model has proven very effective is in the labor and delivery room. Is the labor coach's role to actually "have the baby?" Of course not. That remains the woman's work. Does the coach play a meaningful role? You betcha! The coach provides support and encouragement. She or he can help the mother to focus on breathing techniques and other skills that facilitate the birthing process. The coach stands powerfully in this space as the mother's partner, helping her through the rough spots, and is the first to celebrate progress and achievement.

Other disciplines have also successfully used the coaching model with great results. The arts, such as acting, drama, and voice coaching; the fitness industry, through personal training; even the military utilizes coaches. They have all adopted the coaching model because it works in delivering results. And that is exactly what makes it so attractive in business.

There is a growing body of evidence, both qualitative and quantitative (story and statistics), that demonstrates that coaching

- Is one of the most straightforward ways to create and sustain full-throttle engagement
- Achieves organizational strategies and goals
- Aids in the development of healthy, vibrant experiences at work
- Contributes to talent planning by attracting, cultivating, and keeping world-class people
- Positions us all to see ourselves as capable leaders who hold ourselves accountable for greatness

Unfortunately, some of us have had a bad experience with someone who called themselves a coach or who said that they were "coaching" us. When I feel people pushing away the idea of coach leadership, I have found that it is almost always related to misuse, mislabeling, or misunderstanding of the coaching approach and its skills, tools, and techniques.

Here are some of the ways I have found coaching to be maligned:

1. Someone told me that, in their organization, coaching means that "your boss is yelling at you for not doing what she told you." This is an immediate tip off that the organization or a particular person does not understand some very fundamental elements, the basics, of coaching.

2. When I hear workers say that coaching doesn't feel any different than being told what to do, I know that there is something out of whack, because it is markedly different than managing. The terms are not interchangeable.

3. One organization re-named their disciplinary process "coaching" without changing its basic intent or the process. Can you imagine what workers thought of coaching in that organization? Do you think that their response changed simply because of a superficial name change?

4. Occasionally, I'll hear that coaching means that everyone gets away with everything or that anything goes in an organization. That is so far from a true coaching model that it scares me.

If you have had an experience with coaching in the workplace that has been less than productive or that left you disappointed, discouraged, or disillusioned, I ask that you do your best to set that feeling aside, suspend your past experiences, wipe the slate clean and see coaching through a new, fresh lens. Who knows, you could be the person to help your organization shift its practices and rethink its definition of engagement and leadership!

As a business and leadership coach, I often speak to large groups of people as well as facilitate learning programs on organizational transformation and how to be an effective coach leader. No matter the venue, however, I always encounter another reaction at about this same point in the discussion. Some of my colleagues who have worked long and hard to complete their business degrees get this sinking feeling in the pit of their stomachs and I can understand this major push back. It comes from a place of fear and doubt. Inevitably someone asks, "Are you suggesting that we should put our well-honed management skills on the organizational shelf?"

My answer is always "no!" Rather, as the way that we do business changes dramatically, I believe that we are being challenged to more narrowly focus those management skills.

One of my organizational mantras is, "Manage things—coach people!" So, knock yourself out managing budgets, inventories, projects, facilities, schedules, etc., with a new appreciation that even these left-brained elements may need to be re-created to encourage partnership. When it comes to people, decide to coach all of those around you and be willing to be coached yourself so that everyone can reach their personal bests.

For those of you who still think managing people is more effective than coaching them, consider the following:

- First and foremost, coaching is a straightforward pathway to full-throttle engagement that can be universally learned and used by all organizations and by all people in those organizations.

- From our learning in Chapter 1, there is an increasingly persuasive body of evidence that suggests that the expectations of our American workforce are changing. As a result of this desire for a different work experience, and all of the other dynamics that we highlighted, managing people is working less well and is far less attractive or acceptable than it was even ten short years ago. Managing people instead of coaching them falls into the leadership model that gets wrong-er and wrong-er with each passing month or year.

- In addition to the fact that managing people is less of a fit for the work force, it also requires ongoing oversight and frequent intervention. This traditional leadership model assumes that such oversight and intervention is required to assure that everyone does what they are supposed to do. With flatter organizational structures which include fewer managers to make sure that the work gets done, the entire model of management is increasingly unsuccessful. Also, too frequently, the old model of managing people has exactly the opposite effect. Parent-child dynamics flourish, dysfunctional comfort reigns, and we wait to be told what to do. To cope, too many of us adopt a bunker mentality and turf wars surface.

- Managing people also typically places team members in a "one down" or subordinate position. This does not result in allowing others to be at their very best at work. In fact, it sends the perhaps unintended message that "management does not think that non-managers can choose to hold themselves accountable and be responsible." This breeds what is called a "culture of compliance," but that definitely will *not* carry us forward into the Conceptual Age.

- Management also tends to focus almost exclusively on the end or the results. While a successful outcome is critical to a successful business, it is not the only vital factor. Paying attention to the means, the "how," is equally important when it comes to assisting people in motivating themselves to greatness, living their signature strengths, and making a unique contribution.

- Finally, coaching works better! Here are some compelling "fast facts" that make the case:
  - It is often reported in the business press that over half of Fortune 500 companies use coaching as part of their success strategy.
  - The Manchester study of the effectiveness of coaching found a ROI (return on investment) of six to one. What that means is that organizations who invest in learning how to become an organization full of coach leaders can expect an average ROI of six dollars for every dollar spent! Now, that's a WOW experience.
  - That same Manchester study found that 77 percent of professionals working with a business coach or working in coaching cultures reported improved relationships with their direct reports; 71 percent with their boss; and 63 percent with their peers. As we have learned, rich

relationships in the workplace translate directly to many and varied measures of success.[16]

◻ Coaching is an embedded part of the culture at Motorola, where the ROI has been reported to be as high as twenty-nine to one! [17]

What possibility coach leadership holds!

Coach Leader Defined

If coach leadership is different than managing and/or directing people, and it offers the primary route for all of us to practice full-throttle engagement and lead from our seats, then what exactly is it? What are the key distinctions that make it so different and so useful in creating engaged workplaces?

Here is my simple definition of coach leadership:

*Coach leadership is a way of interacting with another (or others) that promotes improvement and development. In other words, it brings about or contributes to positive change, primarily **through the will of the other person(s)** rather than simply out of obedience to me or you or even "them." Great coach leaders believe wholeheartedly that there is brilliance in everyone and they understand just as wholeheartedly that the primary responsibility of coach leaders is to assist others in accessing their own brilliances, their own answers, and then taking inspired action from there to get the work done well. When practiced more and more universally in an organization, by more and more people at more and more levels, coach leadership is the fuel that powers full-throttle engagement. And this fuel is completely renewable and resides in abundant supply within all of us.*

While coach leadership is quite simple, it is not at all easy for many of us to carry in our head, heart, and gut day in and day out because it has not been our habit to do so. It requires a significant shift in our individual and team patterns. It definitely takes lots of unlearning and involves a good measure of risk taking and belief. Above all, it takes tenacity to keep it going when things inevitably get tough.

It is so powerful and so effective because, at its core, it is a fundamental belief that the other person is capable, smart, and talented adult willing to contribute. Coach leadership rides on the firm belief that the person who is closest to the actual work often "knows best," which means that they have the answers to the problem they face; they just need the space in which to find it, express it, and put it into action.

As coach leaders, we must hold the other person in "unconditional positive regard," a marvelous phrase coined by Thomas Crane.[18] The primary gift of coach leadership is the embedded challenge to create our own solutions. To accomplish that, everyone needs the permission and the space to allow that to happen. Decision making is de-centralized and pushed throughout the organization to absolutely everyone.

Stop for a moment and truly consider the implications of that claim. The gift of coach leadership is that it promotes an organizational culture in which everyone routinely is an everyday leader, leading powerfully and fully from their seat.

One of my favorite quotes captures this so perfectly:

Change done by me is an opportunity.
Change done to me is a threat.
All change looks like failure in the middle.
—Lizbeth Moss Kantor

Coach leadership feels like "change done by me" more often than not because it calls on each of us to make decisions, to be active problem solvers and take charge adults, rather than passive "Stepford-like" human resources. More stuff gets done "by me" and that is an opportunity. Coaching happens inside relationships, in real conversations between success partners. Instead of telling or directing or "bossing" someone around, coaching demands that we create solutions and move forward through collaborative inquiry (sometimes called appreciative inquiry) which means that we are working together to ask the right questions that will lead to viable solutions.

As coach leaders, we coach with rather than to. We ask and answer high quality questions together aimed at accessing options, alternatives, fresh perspectives, laser focused insights, and BFOs (blinding flashes of the obvious). Coaching is an effective way of being together at all levels within an organization and in all interactions. As coach leaders, we want the best for each of our colleagues as much as we want that for ourselves. By its very nature, it creates leaders around you at all levels and layers of the organization.

In order to be effective as coach leaders, both people (or all people) in the dialogue both teach and learn in the rhythm of everyday conversations. In this type of situation, everyone understands that there will be times when they take the lead and there will be times when they follow someone else's lead. Coach leadership cracks open the door for some of the most productive brainstorming I've ever witnessed because it is done collaboratively (yes, there's that word again). Everyone is included in strategy, planning, and goal setting.

As coach leaders, those with traditional leadership titles challenge their team members to find their own solutions, take charge of projects or tasks, and go beyond the average. The traditional leader learns how to get out the way and let their team members step up and take responsibility for the work that's been handed to them. For that effort, the traditional leader rewards independent and innovative thinking and behaving; they are willing to share power and authority. And they get the importance of celebrating. These leaders stop acting like parents, wardens, know it alls, or dictators.

When universal coach leadership is practiced, staff members and/ or team members step up. They stop waiting to be told what to do. They take risks by offering solutions, speaking up, and telling the truth. They become constructive, going well beyond the minimum. They stop acting like children, victims, cynics, and I-told-you-so's.

At the most fundamental level of language, coaching is not about "I" or "you" or "them" but about "we." We assist each other in identifying obstacles so as to move more easily and quickly around them and get on with the business of co-creating a great place to work. We collectively keep our eyes on the overall good of the entire organization instead of a narrow focus on getting our tasks done. We ask questions and listen in order to expand our perspectives and surface up more and different solutions and new opportunities. We keep the focus to insure success.

There is a saying that is often attributed to Lao Tzu: "Feed a man a fish, feed him for a day. Teach him how to fish and feed him for a lifetime." Coach leadership is closely aligned with the latter. If we assist one another to have the courage and the will to look within for solutions; if we get out of each other's way so that we can take chances, learn, grow, and lead, then we will stand a much improved chance of having what we say we all want: an engaged, energetic workforce; a team who holds themselves accountable with peak performance and the results to prove it.

In this way, you can view coach leadership as a way of being and acting, something that is:

- All about change.
- Moving from where we are today to where we want to be next.
- An organic, holistic process—not a gimmick, not the program of the month, and certainly not an "intervention" for troubled employees.
- Used by everyone. It is 360-degrees around the organization—coaching up, down, and across in an organization. But it is also coaching within by skillfully coaching ourselves.
- Based on a powerful belief that each of us has almost all of the answers within us and that what we need to access them is a success partner who believes in us and can assist us in holding the frame of possibility.

Coach leadership is as much about unlearning as it is about learning. Businesses in the know gravitate towards it because it is absolutely results driven. Any "coaching" resource that says otherwise isn't coaching. Coach leadership challenges. It demands the best. It's edgy and risky. It's big and bold.

Coaching offers a platform for surfacing up limiting beliefs, old programs, and patterns and allows us to shift them. To do that requires us to connect not just to logic, but to intuitive intelligence and emotional intelligence as well.

When it's done well, coach leadership becomes a portal for adding incredible clarity and vision to one's work because it is supported by built-in accountability.

Above all, it is a way of "being" at work. You are a coach leader all the time, so it is not just a technique, but a fundamental way of acting and communicating in a work relationship. It is a way to create and tend meaningful relationships in the workplace that fosters community and *requires that **everyone lead from their seat!***

While the possibilities that coaching offers are enormous and hugely exciting, it is also equally important that we identify what coach leadership is *not*.

- Coach leadership is not the same as mentoring—A pure mentoring model is similar to the relationship between teacher and pupil. Or master to apprentice. The mentor shares his/her approach with the mentee. I call it a "download from the divine." And the mentee is expected to follow the prescribed way of the mentor or master. In the last decade, the line between mentoring and coaching has become blurred and often the terms are used interchangeably.

- Coach leadership is not therapy. The coaching framework and the success partnership that is developed lends itself to breakthroughs, new insights, a surge forward, surrendering old habits, and much more. As a coach leader, we recognize that our point of power is in the present, with implications for the future. The coach leader is not, however a trained mental health professional in most cases. When we suspect that someone may have needs that go beyond coaching, we each have an obligation to tell the other person. Many organizations have effective EAP programs (employee assistance programs) for these situations. Make yourself smart and learn about your organization's resources today.

- Coach leadership is so not a parent-child exchange. Coaching is compassionate and empathetic, but it is not about "care-taking." As coach leaders, we don't need to protect others or falsely reassure them.

We also do not need to tell them what to do. This leads to a group of people who become dependent and do not see it as their job to be responsible for their own future and the future of the organization. As I have said before, the parent-child dynamic is closely aligned with that old patriarchic model of the Industrial Age. Coach leadership is not mothering. It is not babysitting. This caretaking approach is simply a form of control. Remember, feed a man a fish....

- Coach leadership is absolutely not manipulation. The intention that we must hold in our hearts and heads is that we believe in our colleagues; we want them to be successful and powerful within themselves; and that they have most of the answers they need to be great. That means that we do not use the coaching model to solicit only our preferred solution or response.

- Coach leadership is also not a magic bullet. It is about being in the right relationship with others in your organization and that takes time, energy, and attention.

- Coach leadership is not a "re-branding" opportunity. It is not a new label for an old way of being together. Don't insult your colleagues by re-packaging old management approaches and calling it coaching. It is fundamentally different than managing, directing, prescribing or browbeating. It is also not begging or cajoling.

- Coach leadership is not simply a tool. There is a science to coaching and, as such, there are techniques and tools that help us to refine our coaching skills. There is also an artful or intuitive component to coaching as well.

- Coach leadership is not merely an intervention. It isn't something that you keep in your hip pocket and pull out when something or someone has gotten derailed. You live it every day. It is a way of interacting that inevitably leads us to full-throttle engagement.

- Coach leadership is not something that only management uses. It is a way of being that is practiced universally, by everyone. It is in the DNA of an organization. It's under our skin as we embed it at a cellular level. Thinking of it as just another management tool diminishes it and may prevent you from playing big in your organization.

Your job and your organization are increasingly complex. Fundamental change is the norm, not the exception. Influencing without direct authority is critical. And there aren't enough hours in the day. So we all need to be an extraordinary leader, regardless of position or title. And to be that leader, you need to be a coach leader.

Consider this:

— At 211 degrees, water is hot.

— At 212 degrees, water boils.

— And with boiling comes steam.

— And steam powers locomotives.

— One extra degree makes all the difference in life & business.

— One degree of effort makes the difference between good and great.

— Coaching has the potential to give you that extra degree. Exceed expectations in a memorable way. Be not good but great and watch the power real engagement holds for you and your organization.

Coaching TO GO

Still hungry for more learning? Want to make the learning stickier? Try these on for size to expand your perspective and turn knowledge into power!

1. **Must haves for your professional library**—Jamie and Maren Showkeir have written a provocative, intelligent, and impactful book entitled, *Authentic Conversations*. Even though the authors rarely, if ever, reference the coaching framework, it is, for me, one of the best books on the language of coaching. It would be a great choice for a shared read with your teammates. I also recommend reading *Masterful Coaching* by Robert Hargrove. It is so well written, offers a thorough overview of the coaching model and makes a compelling case for considering coaching as the breakthrough tool in business today. Finally, I recommend *The Heart of Coaching* by Thomas Crane. It emphasizes the relationship aspect of coaching and gives some meaningful tips, tools, and techniques.

2. **Check out the Rose Story**—If we are to become more masterful coach leaders, then most of us must fundamentally shift our thinking about the people around us at work. We need to begin to think of each other as capable, smart, talented, creative, willing, and accountable. Visit www.vantage-inter.com and read the Rose Story for some fresh insight in this area. It takes about two minutes and may bring a smile to your face. And it may help embed this new thinking just a bit more.

3. **Create your own comparison**—Here's a terrific exercise that can be personalized and deliver major insights. Create your own chart comparing coaching and managing. Think of how you handle situations throughout the day. Write down verbs to describe your actions. Now, ask yourself if each of them is more closely aligned with the coach leader model or the old management model. This can be helpful regardless of your current title or position. Write down what you learned from the exercise and what you will do differently moving forward.

4. **Scenario**—Here's a brief scenario to consider. Based upon our learning so far, create two different endings—one assuming that it is an engaged organization with coach leaders at all levels and the next assuming that it is a very traditional organization with a rigid top-down hierarchical approach. Discuss what you learn with your colleagues, at a staff meeting or an in-service program.

    One of your colleagues, Dave, is struggling in his position. The new pace and increased demands in the organization seem to be more than he can handle right now. On the surface, things appear to be okay. But you have experience and evidence that clearly point to multiple major challenges within his division. You are not the only one to see what's happening. You have had confidential conversations with mutual colleagues. One of them described the situation as, "watching a train wreck happen in slow motion." You have hinted to Dave that you see what is happening. He looks nervous, but discounts the problems. The only person who doesn't seem to know what's going on behind the scenes is the Vice President, to whom you and Dave both report. Part of you thinks that it is her responsibility to recognize this and address it with Dave. Another part of you believes that you should be more assertive in conversation with Dave. Finally, there is a small part of you that feels as though it is not your j-o-b to get involved. What do you do as an engaged coach leader? What would you do if your organization were very much oriented to the "chain of command?"

Notes:

Intentionality:

A Portal For The Extraordinary

How many people are trapped in their everyday habits;
part numb, part frightened, part indifferent?
To have a better (work) life,
we must keep choosing how we are living.
—Albert Einstein

You are searching for the magic key that will unlock the door to the
source of power; and yet you have the key in your own hands, and you
may use it the moment you learn to control your own thoughts.
Napoleon Hill—*Think and Grow Rich*

For many of us, the coach leader model is not yet who we are today in the workplace. To be a coach leader means that we're seeing ourselves as one another's success partners. We actively participate in someone else's discovery, growth, and change process by asking questions that help that person to access his/her own answers.

Being a coach leader may feel foreign, scary, weak, or downright wrong. It may even feel threatening to those of us in "management positions" as we ask ourselves what value we contribute if we aren't "telling people what to do and making sure that they do it." While it may be exhilarating to some, it might be downright uncomfortable for team members to realize that they have an active role to play in helping themselves, their colleagues, and their entire organization to succeed.

To be a coach leader, to take ourselves that one extra degree from good to great, to move ourselves forward and away for good from the old "command and control" model left over from the Industrial Age requires some sort of fuel, something to move us from point a to point b.

It needs to be powerful, this fuel, for us to reach our goal of always achieving strong outcomes while allowing all the members of the organizations to choose to be happy and productive along the way. And fortunately for us, this fuel has been with us all along. It is buried within ourselves and has everything to do with how successful we are or not and has everything to do with how we think about even the smallest details of our work and our lives.

In order to be an effective coach leader and have full engagement, we must become increasingly **aware** of our thoughts, feelings, and behaviors. This allows us to step back from a situation, assess the problem and figure out how to help without stepping on anyone's toes.

Becoming more aware of how we think and behave has a very nice side effect: we become more **choiceful** about what we're doing or saying. Choiceful means that we're constantly aware of the choices we're making in all our actions and interactions with others.

What allows us to be more aware and choiceful in the way we think, feel, and act is **intentionality.** Intentionality, which at its heart means that we are acting and thinking with intention, with purpose, is the fuel that keeps us moving along so that we can grow and become masters in our work lives. I actually have come to think of intentionality as this:

Becoming aware of and then choosing our thoughts,
feelings, beliefs, and actions on a regular basis.

If you are working on your thoughts, feelings, beliefs, and actions on a regular basis with a purpose, then you are living with intentionality.

Dysfunctional Comfort Explained

Intentionality is a simple concept, but not easy to practice day in and day out. We have come to live so much of our day on autopilot. We get to work, we open our inbox, we move on with our day looking at the clock too many times because we want the day to be over so our "real life" can begin. Or, conversely, we can come up for air from our whirlwind of a day only to find that it's 6:00 p.m. and we get that sick feeling in our stomachs because we haven't checked a single item from our To Do list.

If we are to challenge our current habits at work when we interact with one another, then we must come off autopilot—stop thinking, feeling, or doing things only because we have thought, felt or acted that way for a very long time.

To be an effective coach leader, one of the first steps we must take is to develop a healthy mistrust for our current habits. Many of us cling to the familiar like a life preserver in turbulent waters. We are comfortable with what we know even if we suspect or know that it doesn't come close to being us at our best.

My language for the organizational quicksand that holds many of us stuck is dysfunctional comfort. I have mentioned this term before, but in its fullest sense, it refers to that odd feeling of reassurance or relief around a longstanding relationship, process, procedure, or approach even though it is unhealthy, outmoded, broken, or just plain wrong. We are reassured simply because it is familiar. It includes old thought patterns (prejudices and biases) about other people, groups, or institutions that are kept alive in organizations despite a contrary objective truth. Dysfunctional comfort also has a complementary feeling of defensiveness when we are asked to surrender it for something different. Dysfunctional comfort is the archenemy of intentionality. And, because of that, it stands squarely in the way of leading from every seat and full-throttle engagement.

Why is dysfunctional comfort so seductive?

In my learning programs, I always ask participants to voice some of the reasons why they think they hang on to dysfunctional comfort for so long. Here are some of the answers we've come up with:

1. **My reptilian brain makes me do it!**—A powerful part of the brain, the amygdala, wants the world to run on routine, not change. This ancient area of the mind deals with the way we perceive and respond to the world; the amygdala urges us to favor the familiar and routine. It craves safety and control. At some point in the distant past, this may have saved our species from extinction. Today, however, it is maladaptive. We are not simply servants of our amygdala! We can choose to intentionally over ride this tendency and begin to see sparks of possibility for making things better around us, including ourselves.

2. **Inertia has me in its grip**—It's easier to know what to expect and complain about what is wrong than to hold oneself accountable for identifying challenges and finding better solutions for them. It takes energy to get going in a different (even slightly) direction. We've got to climb out of our thought rut and intentionally engage in something new.

3. **The devil you know is better than the one you don't**—There's a classic line by Woody Allen: "Everyone wants to go to heaven, but no one wants to die." When asked, most employees will agree that they want things to get better in the workplace; yet few are willing to be the change that they want to see. The possibility that things might actually get worse looms large for some.

4. **I'll settle for good**—I frequently find that our colleagues convince themselves that, while something isn't the best that it could be, it's also not the worst. "It's a whole lot worse in other organizations!" "It's never going to be perfect!" or "don't wake that baby to hear it cry!" are examples of excuses to keep doing what we're doing. This often feels as though it is a particularly reasonable position to take in light of the hectic pace and degree of "busyness" that many of us experience in our work lives. "Good," as Jim Collins so astutely reminds us, "is the enemy of great."[19]

In order to break free from the cycle of dysfunctional comfort and engage in more and more intentionality, we must begin to cultivate uncomfortableness as a cultural value in ourselves, others around us, and throughout our organizations. We must reconsider it as a healthy part of the growth and development process of individuals, teams, and organizations.

If you begin to first raise your level of awareness and become more mindful of what is going on around you and then begin to see those same circumstances and events through a different lens, you will undoubtedly pick up on new options, fresh possibility, unexplored opportunities, or alternate solutions.

Come up out of the weeds—the never ending list of tasks that consume your day—and see things hidden in plain sight. Check out this chapter's *Coaching TO GO section* for a great video on "inattentional blindness." It makes this point in a powerful way!

We don't see things as they are. We see things as we are.
—The Talmud

To live and work with intentionality means we've got to start questioning everything, but because being a coach leader is not our current habit or pattern, we must become very mindful about what we do every minute of our day in order to begin and complete the process of shedding an old way of being and donning a new one. Remember, a snake must shed her skin from time to time or die. Once the skin has been shed, the snake is not weaker or more vulnerable, but renewed and stronger. Shed or dead. I think the same is true for us.

We must shed same-old, same-old thinking! I guarantee that if you do, your personal and professional lives will improve. I have never seen it fail.

The Mantra of Intentionality

One of the most powerful tools that I have used to become more intentional and then sustain the made changes is outlined below. It is four simple words that, together, create a rhythmic mantra (here, mantra means "words repeated to aid concentration and focus") that I repeat over and over again to remind myself that I am in charge of me at all times, even when things look like they're not going my way. Here is that mantra:

REFRAME

RECLAIM

REJOICE

RE-CHOICE

Here is what those words mean to me:

Reframe—I can choose the frame of reference that I use in situations.

Reclaim—I am powerful in my experiences. I will choose my thoughts, feelings, and behaviors. I won't turn my power over to other people, circumstances, or events. I reclaim my personal power.

Rejoice—There is an awful lot going well in my experience at any given time. I will notice and celebrate those things. I will choose to be appreciative.

Re-choice—Throughout my day, I will actively remember that I choose my reactions and responses. I will be intentional and purposeful when choosing. I will not simply be on autopilot!

I have repeated these to myself so often that I swear they are now embedded in my DNA. They serve as my framework for intentionality.

And they also remind me of something equally as powerful and empowering. While I believe that we are entirely in charge of our own thoughts, feelings, beliefs, and actions, I am also equally clear that I am not in charge of anyone else's. I cannot make someone else happy, for example. I can foster an environment that is helpful. I can encourage that person. But in the end, it is their choice to be happy.

In order to be most effective, we must focus our attention within what Dr. Stephen Covey calls our circle of influence as opposed to things outside of our control—a circle of concern.[20]

This simple, elegant concept always reminds me that there are things over which we have total control; some things over which we only have some control; and then finally there are those things over which we have no control. The best part is the realization that we can choose to let go of things we can't control. Worrying or fretting about these things or attempting to "force" something to happen, does little good. Instead, let's remain fanatically focused on all of the things that we have almost complete control over—our thoughts, our feelings, our attitudes, our behaviors, our words, our body language.

How do we begin to become more mindful of our thoughts, feelings, beliefs, and actions? I challenge you, even dare you, to pursue a mastery plan to become more intentional!

Consider the following tips, tools, and techniques that have worked with the many of my clients to jump start your work around intentionality:

1. **You are here**—Just as maps in malls help you to identify exactly where you are in the moment, I encourage you to try an interesting albeit unscientific exercise to determine your dominant thoughts—where you choose to hold your thoughts, feelings and actions throughout the typical workday. Pick a work day, any day, and from the moment that you awaken until you crawl into bed that night, periodically (say, every fifteen minutes) take specific note of what you are thinking, feeling, and how you are behaving. Without assigning any judgment to it. You may find this truly illuminating. I personally took this challenge many years ago when a colleague offered it to me. I was fairly dismissive of it initially. After all, I am an optimist, constructive and generally self-aware. I was confident that I would end up affirming that self-impression. So, I picked a day and was surprised when, at 5:15 a.m. on my way to the gym, only moments after waking up, I found myself yelling at the only other car on the interstate because he was in "my" lane! The rest of the day

yielded lots of new insights and opportunities for learning. Take the challenge and find out where you are today. No matter where you are today, you can become more intentional tomorrow and create more useful habits.

2. **Unlearn**—Many of us turn over our personal power to other people, circumstances, events, etc. We have bought into the myth that someone else is in control of our thoughts or feelings. For example, *"s/he made me so frustrated!"* You may have chosen to be frustrated by something that someone else said or did but they did not make you have that feeling. If you want to be frustrated, then do so. It is your choice. Determine how long you will stay there—also your choice. And simply know that you are not at your best as long as you stay there. I can honestly say that I no longer have bad days. I have bad moments from time to time but not a full day. I choose. Always.

3. **Reformat your old programs**—The past does not necessarily predict the future. You get to decide how to be and what to do. Reset your subconscious to a new channel of self-talk (Dr. Phil refers to this as old programs or old tapes). The most important conversation that you have every day as a coach leader is with yourself! Create an inner coach and begin to pay attention to what your best self has to say. Silence your inner gremlin. Visualizing, using micro-affirmations, (small ways in which you validate yourself and recognize that you are "perfect enough") and journaling are also excellent tools to help you to shed same-old, same-old habits and create and keep new ones. This is not as easy as some books and products make it appear. Some of our habits have been with us for a while (years and years for some) and actually served us well at one point in time. Sometimes they have been around so long that they feel like the truth or the way that it must be. It requires energy, attention, and a desire to shift.

4. **Pre-pave your day**—Faithfully use the technique of top performers in all fields, yours included. Visualize the various segments (for example, meetings, conversations, interviews,

projects) of your work day as you would ideally like to experience them. Stephen Covey identified this as one of the "seven habits of highly effective people." He called it "beginning with the end in mind."[21] We are more likely to have an outcome similar to the one we ideally want by focusing our thoughts and emotions on it before it happens. Thoughts become things!

One of my coaching clients has used this mini skill to completely reframe his participation in meetings throughout his business day. Before he enters the meeting room, he simply pauses and reflects on who he wants to be during that meeting, how he will behave, and what outcome he wants. Then he keeps those thoughts foremost in his mind as he moves through the meeting. Nothing else changed...and yet everything changed for this leader.

5. **Collect positive aspects**—Focus intentionally on what is right about people, situations, etc. As coach leaders, we want to work toward focusing 80 percent of our time, energy, and attention on enhancing our own greatness and our signature strengths, and only 20 percent on lesser strengths or weaknesses. The same success formula applies to how we choose to view and interact with others. I read somewhere that when we focus intently on our "weaknesses" we simply build strong weaknesses. Because coaching is a strength—or brilliance—based way of being in relationship with others at work, mastering this aptitude is vital stage on our journey toward intentionality.

6. **Participate in a mastermind group**—In the book, *The Leadership Secrets of Jesus,* we are encouraged to "pay any price to remain in the company of extraordinary people."[22] To make new habits as sticky as possible and to assure that they "take" or replace our old habits, intentionally spending time with like-minded colleagues is a worthy strategy. Create your own or join one of the thousands of groups available, in person or virtually.

7. **A simple "how to" approach**—Do what Joe Vitale and many authors and experts advocate to approach any situation, relationship, project, challenge, or opportunity with greater measures of intentionality:

a. Know exactly what it is that you do *not* want in this situation, in vivid Technicolor detail. Write it down. Many get stuck here but not you!

b. Know exactly what it is that you *do* want, in rich detail. Don't censor yourself. Tell the whole story. Paint the entire picture.

c. Identify exactly what is currently in your way from experiencing what it is that you want. List everything! Shine the light on those old programs, gaps in resources, etc. Think about what is under your control to change. Then commit to addressing these things.

d. Identify how you will feel when you have exactly what it is that you want. Start to feel those feelings now, to the best of your ability.

e. Get moving in the right direction. Name three actions that you can take to move you forward.[23]

6. **Have a daily intentionality practice**—Embed intentionality throughout your work day. Make it a part of your DNA. This is a keystone for the inner journey that we all must take to undergo the transformation to coach leader. Here is an example for your consideration:

a. Borrow my energizing practice of beginning your day with "raging appreciation." Find ten things for which you are truly grateful. They can be large or small.

b. Read your vision for yourself each day and visualize living that vision for no more than five minutes each day. Don't have a personal/professional vision, strategies, and goals for yourself? What an opportunity—create one!

c. Create a series of affirmations that are uniquely you. An affirmation is a present tense positive statement of a circumstance that you want to create. Play them in your mind throughout the day. Replace all of the other "head trash" you may have floating through your mind BI (before intentionality).

d. Pause before the primary segments of your day—meetings, conversations, project work—and pre-pave it as was discussed above.

e. At the end of your day, look back and list the many things that worked or went right that day. I call it evidence journaling. Note all of the evidence that things are working in your experience. You would not believe what ends up in mine!

6. **Use your Xena tools**—A number of years ago, there was a campy, yet oddly intriguing TV show called *Xena: Warrior Princess*. It was set in the Middle Ages and was all about the adventures of Xena and her side-kick, Gabrielle. These two women were a medieval female Batman and Robin pair who triumphed over evil. Xena had great tools. One of my favorites was her bracelets. (Note: Wonder Woman had great bracelets too!) She could simply raise her arm(s) and her bracelets would deflect lightning bolts, incoming weapons…well, you get the idea. I think that we can use this fun image to remind ourselves to deflect negativity and anything else that could derail us from being intentional. Get those bracelets up!

Here are a few examples of how people just like you have successfully used intentionality to create different experiences at work:

□ *The manager of a branch office of a large bank used intentionality practices to stop immediately telling people what they should do and attempting to solve all of their problems. Now, she pauses, listens, asks questions, and expects people to have solutions of their own.*

□ *A cafeteria cashier shifted from hating her job, feeling invisible and unappreciated and disliking the people whom she served, to really connecting and helping people get their day off to a great start. She decided to make one small change— she would smile more at people. That's it. Big doors swing on small hinges. Little change…big payoff. In less than a month, she was receiving many complements and one of her regular customers told her that she should change her name to Joy, because that's what gift she gave everyone. It is also important to note that the restaurant's business in the morning began to grow. Coincidence? I don't believe in them!*

◻ *A brave IT manager approached his COO and told him that several timelines for crucial projects were unrealistic. He had data to back up his claim. His COO listened, primarily because the IT manager had very intentionally chosen his words and his body language; and showed up with an alternate strategy. That's leading from your seat! That's being different and better. And it worked. And it changed that person's relationship with the COO for good.*

◻ *Union workers and management staff at a manufacturing company set aside long standing distrust and began to communicate differently. There were only small wins at first. It was so hard for both sides to stop repeating unproductive behavior—dysfunctional comfort—and start thinking about what might be possible. Instead of blaming, there's more ownership. They have much more work to do together, but let's declare it a victory so far.*

Being a coach leader and leading from your seat in your organization is probably a different way of being for most of us. That means that we will need to practice intentionality in who we choose to show up as each day and in our everyday interactions. It's not enough to show up and do your *j-o-b*. If we want to have a better future together at work, then we need to generate "sparks of possibility" in our organizations.

In *The Art of Possibility*, Ben and Roz Zander share a memorable story that highlights how fundamentally important this attitude is:

In the Middle Ages, when lighting a fire from scratch was a difficult process, people often carried a metal box containing a smoldering cinder and kept it alive throughout the day with little bits of kindling. This meant that a man could light a fire with ease wherever he went, to meet the basic needs of warmth, protection and cooking. He always carried a spark.[24]

We have, at our finger tips, infinite capacity to light a spark of possibility in ourselves and others through the power of coach leadership.

Believe that others are eager to catch the spark and be prepared to do likewise. Be a spark in your organization!

Coaching TO GO

1. **Must haves for your professional library**—Here is a list of the books that I have found to be of most value in understanding and then practicing "intentionality."

   The Power of Intention by Wayne Dyer, PhD

   If How-to's were Enough, We'd all be Skinny, Rich and Happy by Brian Klemmer

   Infinite Possibilities by Mike Dooley

   The Other 90 Percent by Robert Cooper

2. **View the video**—There is a powerful little video on "inattentional blindness" that captures the essence of intentionality so well. Very interesting; created the "aha!" moment. Visit the vantage website to check it out: www.vantage-inter.com. Or view it on Youtube.

3. **Take the leadership dare**—Check in on where you choose to hold our thoughts and feelings regularly. Pick a day (any work day will do) and for that day, I want you to simply notice what you are thinking and feeling throughout the day. Mind you, I don't want you to change a thing for this exercise. Simply notice! Every fifteen minutes or so, note what you were thinking and feeling. At the end of the day, take a look at the pattern of your thoughts and feelings. You may be like me; I was surprised to learn how often I was simply on autopilot, not being choiceful about my thoughts and feelings. And, in fact, although I considered myself to be constructive and optimistic, I found that I thought and felt negatively and destructively more often than I was consciously aware.

4. **Visit www.tut.com**—If you are really feeling adventurous when it comes to learning more about intentionality, visit Mike Dooley's intriguing website. It boasts 300,000 regular "adventurers" who are learning more about the powerful force that we

all are in our experience. I am one of them. The daily messages from the universe to which you can subscribe are daily, gentle, fun reminders to become aware and then choiceful about your thoughts.

5. **Try vision boarding**—Because visualization can be such a powerful tool for focusing your thoughts and feelings on a regular basis, many individuals use images and pictures in their intentionality practice. Vision boarding is one such practice. A vision board is simply a large blank space (for example poster board) on which you attach pictures, images, symbols, words, quotes, and other items that have importance to you and relevance for your vision. If you prefer, you can buy a vision board kit on-line. Once you have a completed board, you can display it prominently and spend a short amount of time (about five minutes a day) simply looking at the end results you want to experience. Wow, can this be powerful! To make this more than an exercise, update your vision board regularly and frequently. Keep your vision fresh so that it continues to inspire and delight you. Remain light about visioning. Don't try to make anything happen; simply allow it to happen.

Notes:

5 The "Beingness" of Coaching

We are human "beings" taking inspired actions, not human "doings."
—Leta Beam

Mark Victor Hansen and Roberts Allen in their book, *The One Minute Millionaire,* talk about the importance of being, doing, and having. But they also recognize something very important: "While DOing steps are critical, they are not the first priority, BEing comes first…"

In Chapter 2, I introduced you to my success formula:

BE A LEADER FROM YOUR SEAT

DO COACH WITH EVERYONE AROUND YOU

HAVE FULL-THROTTLE ENGAGEMENT

I also was very clear in that earlier chapter that coaching is the all-important doingness, for if you don't *do* the action, you're not going to have the results. Now's the time to get really clear on the first element of that success formula, the "beingness" of a coach leader, leading from your seat.

While action is pivotal, before anyone can take *inspired* action, we must first focus on who we must "be" as a coach leader in our organization. What I mean by that is we take on the posture, the mannerisms, and the positioning of a coach leader, just as we take on the "beingness" of many roles in our lives: mothers or fathers, friend, daughter, or son. Think about how you simply are in any one of those roles and you'll see that it is quite possible and actually quite easy to adopt the beingness of a coach leader.

How to Be a Coach Leader

For me, our work on intentionality has "warmed the soil" because part of adopting a new way of being requires intention to make it happen. We've got to be aware and then choiceful.

But now, let's talk about the new habits that we must plant, cultivate, and tend in ourselves in order to successfully make the transition from who we are today to who we want to be. Let's focus on becoming more of our best selves. There is nothing in this book that I have not worked on to grow in myself. I have been on a marvelous journey of self-awareness and then mastery for quite a few years. And I can authentically say that I am a very different person than I was in the past. I remain a work in progress, and probably always will. I am constantly evolving and growing and expanding. And at each stage of that growth and development, I appreciate the person that I am and the person that I am on course to become. I wish the same for you in your journey. Enjoy it. Savor it. It's not just about arriving somewhere because we never get this work completely done. But that's okay, for if you aren't growing and learning you are dead!

So, let's call forth the coach leader in all of us! This is intentionality at work. Again, as we have said before, this work is simple but it takes commitment and tenacity to accomplish because it is not currently embedded within us in the form of habits.

Practically speaking, this means that we must first focus on who we want to and need to be in order to be an affirmative participant in the change process. For us, that means that we must "get clear" on who we want to be as a leader and what characteristics and attributes we want to grow in ourselves. Next, we need to intentionally select our self-talk, the most important conversation that we have each day. Finally, we must understand how to allow others to coach us. From there, only after we have initiated that work, we can truly take inspired action and do different things or *do* things differently by coaching. Then we can begin to see the beneficial, different results that we all want: widespread, full-throttle engagement.

The Three Intelligences

First, in order to begin to ignite the spark of coaching within us and then to feed that flame, we need to consciously acknowledge and then intentionally draw from all three of our primary intelligences. Up to this point in workplace experiences, regardless of what we "do" day in and day out, most of us have come to over-rely on our logic or our linear thinking instead of our emotions and our intuition. Now I'm not saying that we throw logic out the window. It's important because in order to be successful at work, we do need to be logical. Coaching, too, is founded in part on logical, linear thinking. But to be a coach leader we can't simply stop there. I think you know by now, logic is not enough. To privilege logic over other kinds of intelligences is part of that old way of thinking and being in the workplace.

Being a coach leader demands that we become integrated thinkers. It requires that we use all means and manner of intelligences—specifically emotional and intuitive, as well as logical. There has been a lot of talk, especially in the last ten years or so, about emotional intelligence, also known as EI. EI is basically the ability to identify, assess, and then use your emotions constructively. But to rely only on EI gets you into as much trouble as only relying on logic.

Integration means that we blend our logic with emotional intelligence as well as intuition. We must connect our heart (emotions), our head (intelligence), and our gut (intuition) in order to become a success partner to our colleagues and our teammates. To do this means we make a bigger difference at work (and frankly in our families and in the community, too).

In fact, to "be" a coach leader and bring the coaching approach to absolutely everything at work, we must actually lead first with our emotions and intuition and then with our logic because, and this is huge, coaching is all about being in relationship with and connected to one another.

No matter what else you get from this chapter, know this: being a coach leader means being in right relationship with ourselves and others. And that means you want as much for the other person(s) as you do for yourself. It's relational first and then logical.

Because we have developed a habit of over-relying on our logic, it can get "bossy" and attempt to dictate how we "should" feel. Unlearn that pattern immediately, but don't throw away logic completely either. Tune into your feelings and your intuition more. Connect with them and then take action from there. When it comes to blending our intelligences, it is our emotions and our intuition that do the integrating. Not our logic.

One of my coaching clients, Bertine McKenna, has a term for this amazing opportunity to connect with ourselves and one another differently by relying on feelings and intuition. She calls it "soul grease." I love it. For her, coaching is about being in community with people at an entirely different level than ever before. And it leads to being heard differently, being more trustful and trustworthy, and it yields different and "better" results.

For me, when we fully and intentionally engage our three intelligences, they create a unique set of circumstances that, in this case, offers an ideal space for everyone to seek out, find, and then bring forth their best selves—in other words to be and do their personal best. Bear in mind, that one's best will be different for different people. Here are the gifts that each of those intelligences brings to the coach leader experience:

Emotion

— connects with others

— assumes that one's own viewpoint is only part of the story

— empathetically see things through someone else's lens

— expresses belief in another

— finds the signature strengths of others and hold up a mirror that allows the other person to see what you see

— shares excitement, energy, and celebration
— collaborates and cross-pollinates
— plays, innovates, and creates
— holds a vision for us, this project or initiative and/or our organization
— challenges prejudices, stereotypes and dysfunctional comfort

Intuition

— senses what to say, when to say it, and how to say it so that our message gets in and lands well with others
— allows us to listen deeply and receive information on another "channel"
— assists us in simply knowing when to ask for more, when to wait, when to be silent, and so forth
— integrates the three intelligences

Logic

— once the emotions and intuition do their work, the logic follows by lining up "inspired" actions to move us and our colleagues forward
— plans, creates checkpoints, and assesses
— attends to the details of "how"

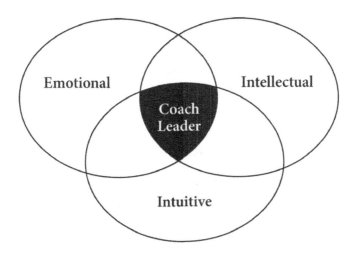

There's another way to look at these three intelligences that's a lot easier to remember and really gets to the heart of the matter. It's this:

HEAD + HEART + GUT = COACH LEADER

Head equals logic; heart, emotions; gut, intuition. That's the being-ness of a coach leader.

Can you see how this can lead to full-throttle engagement? Can you feel and sense how different this is from many traditional models?

Using Head, Heart, and Gut

Using the tips, tools and techniques of intentionality, call forth the coach leader in you! Here's the way that I do it. I:

- Choose how I will feel in any given moment
- Trust my intuition more by quietly and intentionally listening to my best self, my inner coach—that small voice inside me
- Come off auto-pilot and be aware and then intentional
- Am fully present at work. I bring my whole, wonderful, unique self to the experience ad vow each and every day to interact in a way that connects with and supports all others

(And just so you know, I actually wrote this list in the first person because you can use each one of these bullets as an affirmation to affirm your own commitment to being a coach leader).

When you start really taking on the beingness of a coach leader, no matter at what level you reside in an organization, you will find that you become more committed to making a difference for self, colleagues, and the organization. You will discover you are more honest in a way that others can hear and let it in without inviting defensiveness. You work harder toward a bold future for all involved. You become more genuinely engaged in non-stop growth and learning and encouraging others to do the same. You are ready, willing, and able to take inspired action from their new place of being.

Coach Leader Commitments

Coach leaders have what the Buddhists call "crazy wisdom." The way that I understand this idea is a unique blend of wisdom, storytelling/ drama, and boldness. I encourage each of you to rejoice and "re-choice" each day in "being" a coach leader in your workplace community. For me that involves, at a minimum, making a daily commitment to be:

- **An intentional communicator**—Choose your words, your tone of voice, and your body language carefully. Pause before speaking and consider how best to deliver a message that will help you, your colleagues, and your organization to be at their best.

- **Non-judgmental**—Do not rush to judge others. Be intentional about your feelings and remain neutral. Think the best of others. Decide how you will choose to feel knowing that how you feel will, at least in part, determine how things will go.

- **An ego tamer**—Choose to help others be at their best; choose to make a contribution to their greatness; and choose to bring your best self to work for the good of the organization not simply to make yourself look good. While I believe that it is helpful to have a healthy ego and to appreciate ourselves, it does not always have to be about us.

- **Open to new possibilities and options**—As coach leaders, we come to recognize that our way of thinking and being is not the only game in town. We begin to value diversity of thought as a critical factor in creativity, innovation, and continuous quality improvement. If we all thought alike, wouldn't things be boring! We become willing to try new ways of doing things. We entertain the idea that we may not have the whole picture. Even though we have done it "our way" a million times, we are at peace with a new level of understanding there is more than one acceptable way to get us where we need to be.

- **Focused on signature strengths**—Coach leadership is a strength- or "brilliance-" based approach to relationships at work. As a coach, we are called upon to uncover and then uplift our own strengths or brilliances as well as the brilliances of others.

Eighty percent of time, energy, and attention should be focused on knowing and then growing our own and others' brilliances. Only 20 percent of our attention should be focused on what I call lesser strengths (you probably call them weaknesses). To bring out the best in ourselves and others, we must concentrate on what's great about us and them and then accentuate that in all that they do.

- **Willing to surrender the need to "fix" someone or be fixed by someone else**—we are here to support, uplift, and believe in our colleagues. But they are in charge of themselves; we cannot control others. We are only in charge of us! So, focus there and allow others to do their own mastery work. Hold others big in their experience; have high expectations; at the same time, realize that this must be a choice that they intentionally make. The work is still theirs to do. WE must adopt the approach that we and everyone is "perfect enough" where they are today. We are all on our individual life journeys and we need to honor the fact that we can all be in different places. That does not make anyone wrong or inferior, just at a different spot in their evolution of thought.

- **Willing to surrender the outcome**—This can be a challenge for some of us, even more so than some of the other daily commitments to 'being' a coach leader. Surrendering the outcome simply calls upon us to give up the notion that there is only one way (typically our way) to get something accomplished well. Allow others to offer and then attempt different approaches. Do so, not from a place of hoping that they fail and prove that you were right after all, but rather because you want that person(s) to be successful in their own right.

- **Results oriented, not a results machine**—It is not only about the outcome, the destination or the result. The process, the journey is also important. In it resides much learning and growing, excitement and fun, and the opportunity to do good work together. Of course we all want successes; I want them for you. But I frequently challenge my clients by saying that I, as a coach leader, would prefer a bold failure over a mediocre success. Let's not play it too safe; let's try new approaches because that's the innovative process in action. Savor the journey as well as the destination.

The Five Core Values of Coach Leadership

Being a coach leader also means that you intentionally activate five core values, often called dialogue principles, in your own self-talk (dialogues with oneself) and in your interactions with others. These principles are the coaching equivalent to the deep supports that anchor many of our tallest skyscrapers to the bedrock below them. They ground and center us and allow us to develop a robust root system that will support our growth as we become "masterful coaches."

Again, we are shooting here for "perfect enough" rather than perfection. We want to simply begin to "be" different and master this way of being over time as it increasingly becomes our default setting, our habit. Remember, you are only in charge of you; model what you would like to experience from others, regardless of how others choose to be. Embed these dialogue principles in your interactions at work and be prepared to participate in magic as relationships, teams, and the entire workplace community begin to transform:

- **Authenticity**—Because we all are pretty extraordinary with many signature strengths, just attempt to be your best self. The coaching framework is flexible and can accommodate many individual styles. Humor is a big part of who I am as a person. I like having fun and enjoy witty conversations and playfulness. So, as a coach leader, of course those attributes are an important part of who I show up as in interactions. This means that you must really know and appreciate yourself.

- **Inclusion**—This dialogue principle reinforces much of what we have talked about in this chapter. Come to interactions with others with a willingness to consider others' ideas. Value diversity of thought. Differences are not necessarily bad; in fact, they are quite healthy. In interactions, through words, gestures and body language, do what you can to welcome others in.

- **Respect**—This principle is the foundation of civility. You need not agree with someone in order to respect them. If you believe that respect is earned, then at the very least, demonstrate "respectful behavior" by being considerate.

- **Thoughtfulness**—This principle has a double meaning for me. First, I see it as a reminder to be choiceful, intentional with our thoughts. Be aware of how you are thinking and then decide consciously what thoughts will best serve the situation and the people in it. Second, this principle also reinforces the need to be considerate and empathetic to others. Put yourself in their shoes. See things through their eyes.

- **Openness**—This final dialogue principle calls us to identify our prejudices, limiting beliefs, and our "tunnel thinking" that can easily get in the way of authentic coaching conversations and productive relationships.

Finally as a coach leader:

Be…a spark of possibility for yourself and others.

Be…a willing and capable sounding board and thinking partner as others do their work.

Be…the success partner with whom others learn to access the answers that they already have within themselves.

Be…a powerful resource that helps others to reframe their own thinking.

Be…a catalyst for forwarding inspired action.

Coach Yourself—You First!

If you look to lead invest at least 40 percent
of your time coaching yourself—
your ethics, character, principles, purpose, motivation, and conduct.
Invest at least 30 percent coaching those with authority over you, and
15 percent coaching your peers.
Spend the remainder of your time convincing your
"mis-labeled subordinates" to do the same.

—Adapted from Dee Hock

As you begin the work of taking on the beingness of a coach leader, I strongly suggest that you start practicing on yourself.

When I was a kid, my friends and I had a favorite dare: You first! I dare you to begin by applying the coaching approach to your relationship with you.

I firmly believe that coaching allows us all to be at our best. The most critical part of the "inner work" of becoming a coach leader is to, quite literally, coach ourselves. Apply the approach to ourselves. Challenge yourself to live the coaching model out loud. Remember our definition of coaching: a way of interacting that is all about positive change—done through the will of the person involved rather than from a place of compliance or obedience to some authority. Great coaches know that there is untapped potential in everyone and are committed to assisting others in accessing it.

Coach yourself to:

- Embed the five dialogue principles into your everyday approach
- Maintain a heightened level of awareness and confront dysfunctional comfort at every turn by examining your current habits and patterns of being and asking the question: is this me at my best? Is who I am today helping my organization, my team, and my colleagues to shine as brightly as possible? Do not underestimate the intoxicating power of same-old, same-old thinking, feeling, and behaving.
- Create your own powerful coaching space again and again. First thing each day, declare your intention to shed old ways of being and to be more a coach leader.
- Declare your intention "out loud" by sharing it with others and asking them to "coach" you to greatness. Ask them to be your partner.
- Connect your head, heart, and gut intentionally and regularly.
- Choose how you will "be" in more and more interactions. Come off auto-pilot. Stop and think before that meeting, that conversation, that evaluation, etc. Don't be a certain way simply because you have been that way in the past. The past does not necessarily predict the future.

- Be a possibilitarian. Realize that you can be what you want. You and you alone own your thoughts, feelings, and behaviors. Do not turn over control to any person, event or circumstance. When you understand this and begin to practice this in your life, you will become an even more powerful force. You can change. You can grow. You can become.

- Stop expecting others to change first. You are a leader. You lead from your seat. You are responsible for your level of engagement. Worry less about what others are doing or not doing or who they are choosing to be at work.

How to be Coached by Others

The next step in taking on the beingness of a coach leader is crucial. It is also often overlooked because in a way it's the hardest part. Part of the work that is necessary for each of us to become a coach leader and lead from our seat is to be open, receptive, allowing, and even welcoming and appreciative of coaching by others. **All others!** Those who we would consider our bosses; those who are our peers; those who currently report to us; even our "significant others" with whom we regularly interact in the workplace community.

In my twelve-year experience as a leadership and business coach, as well as my time as a corporate employee and executive, I have observed it is most challenging for those who hold "management" positions to accept the gift of coaching from colleagues and mislabeled subordinates. And yet, if we are to move closer to our goal of full-throttle engagement, it is vital that we take seriously the feedback, insights, options, suggestions, and opinions of absolutely everyone with whom we are in relationship.

Up, across, down....coaching is the energy that allows us all to lead from our seats. A room full, a department full, and an organization *full of leaders.*

For those of you who presently hold management positions or who have held such positions in the past, or for anyone who finds that they resist the effort of someone else to coach them, I offer the following disciplines that, when practiced with intentionality, will create the space

to allow others to reach you in a new way and contribute to your growth
and that of your organization:

- **Discipline 1:** Control the tendency to feel defensive. Defensiveness is fear driven. Being in a two-way coaching conversation is
  not an attack. It may be unfamiliar, it may feel uncomfortable.
  But it is useful and meaningful if you allow it to be.

- **Discipline 2:** Tame your ego. If you are used to being the one
  who "runs the show," has all the right answers, or has the last
  word, then routinely turning over power and authority to others can feel like a personal loss or an unfavorable reflection on
  your ability. Intentionally try on for size the possibility that such
  power sharing is a real victory rather than a loss and that it speaks
  volumes about your own self confidence. I believe that you can't
  give some away to others (power, authority, decision making
  responsibility) unless you have it yourself in good measure.

- **Discipline 3:** Slow down to speed up! Yes, you may have a quicker
  answer than someone on your team. And yes, you may have the
  experience to know a solution that will work. But it may not be
  the only way forward. And, forgive me, it may not even be the best
  way. Allowing others to lead from their seat may, particularly in
  the beginning, take longer than simply continuing to tell people
  what to do. Teaching someone how to fish is more time consum-
  ing initially than handing that person a fish to eat. You've got to
  think beyond the short term investment of time. You are allowing
  others to learn and grow and contribute and lead in a different
  way. It's worth the time for a future of full-throttle engagement.

- **Discipline 4:** Fight your tendency to parent or fix others. It's a
  long standing habit for some of us. Recognize it and acknowledge
  it. It is an artifact from that old management model. And it's just
  getting in the way more and more today. As organizations move
  to higher levels of engagement, some in management positions
  begin to wonder whether they still serve a vital role in their organization; whether they are still valued and needed. I have even
  witnessed conscious or unconscious sabotage, passive aggressive

behavior, and dismissiveness in response to these changes. Let me assure you that you continue to be critical to the success of your organization. You are part of the solution. As a coach leader, you teach, challenge, vision, plan, organize, connect, etc. This makes you indispensable.

- **Discipline 5:** Suspend your rush to judgment. I call it remaining "charge neutral." Don't be too quick to dismiss someone else's ideas or feedback solutions. I think every idea, even the very best, is born drowning. We need to get into the habit of throwing ideas a life preserver and see where they take us. Also avoid stereotyping or pigeon holing people. When people in an organization qualify an idea by saying, "consider the source," it usually means that some are viewed as less worthy or less capable and not to be taken seriously.

- **Discipline 6:** Assume that you may not have the whole picture. This is a complement/supplement to Discipline 5. If you make room for the fact that someone else may have a better sense of a situation or a fuller understanding or a clearer view, then you are more receptive to other's input.

- **Discipline 7:** Listen. This is the fundamental coaching skill, but it merits inclusion in these disciplines. Most of us do not self-identify as extraordinary listeners. We're great speakers, debaters, writers, negotiators, persuaders. But listening was not valued in the Industrial Age. And now it is vital to great relationships. It builds people when they feel heard. Not just listening to be polite. Real listening for meaning. We need to listen to learn. We need to listen to innovate. In Chapter 6, you have an opportunity to improve your listening ability as part of the Coaching Starter Kit. Take it! Make it count.

- **Discipline 8:** Be a follower. Following had a bad rap in the Industrial Age. It was seen as weak or less than. Think again! Remember to question these long-standing notions regularly. Practice followership. Reframe it as leadership's positive alter ego. Get good at it. Listen to your intuition to know when to lead and when to follow. Just as dance partners easily flow from following to leading to following, so do success partners flow between the two in everyday interactions. Allow others to be in the shine position more often.

When you have adopted the beingness of a coach leader, the tools and techniques that a coach leader uses will flow more easily. It will make more sense. Taking on the beingness of coach places you in a stronger position to allow the spirit of coaching to shine through each and every exchange throughout your day. It contributes to authenticity. And no matter what happens around you, your experience changes.

Coaching TO GO

1. **Must haves for your professional library**—Here are two resources that may be helpful to you to boost your awareness and understanding of the inner work of coaching.

   Masterful Coaching by Robert Hargrove

   The Heart of Coaching by Thomas Crane

   You Already Know What to Do by Sharon Franquemont

2. **Create a vision board**—I have already introduced you to the concept of vision boarding in the previous chapter. Vision boarding is an interesting tool that is sure to get you out of your left brain logic and more into your creative and intuitive right brain. Revisit #5 in Coaching TO GO in Chapter 4 for directions on how to create a vision board. To help you with the beingness of coaching, begin filling it with images, quotes, powerful phrases, and affirmations of who you want to be in the workplace. Side step the hows for now! Actions, or the doing part, come later. Simply see yourself in different circumstances, surround yourself with micro messages of who you are becoming. This can be great fun and supercharge your own transformation. Give it a try, particularly if it feels very different for you. Remember, we are here shaking our same-old, same-old thinking. We want to challenge our familiar patterns! And, by the way, keep updating your vision board or scrapbook with new stuff. Even inspiring material can become stale after we look at it and review it hundreds of times.

3. **Try new feelings on for size**—Because coaching is driven by feelings and connection, it is helpful to intentionally try new feelings on for size. Here's what I mean by this dare. Right before you begin an interaction, for example a meeting with a colleague with whom you rarely see eye to eye, spend 60 to 90 seconds doing your best to enter into a new feeling space. So, for our example, before the meeting with the colleague, you spend one minute choosing to feel interested in her perspective, appreciating the diversity of thought in your organization, acknowledging her insightfulness, and in general opening up to being a bit optimistic about the outcome of the meeting. Tell yourself that anything is possible, that each interaction is a chance at a fresh beginning, and that the past does not necessarily predict the future, after all, you are in charge of you and you can choose to have a productive interaction. I dare you to try this! If you do, you will be rewarded with a different experience—different by a little or a lot.

4. **Surround yourself with constant reminders**—Organize yourself, your workspace, and your home space so that you surround yourself with reminders of how you are choosing to "be." When you feed yourself a steady diet of fresh, healthy pictures, thoughts, cartoons, and key phrases it has the same effect on our mind and feeling nature as fueling our bodies with a selection of healthy foods.

5. **Engage in a new inner dialogue**—When it comes to choosing to "be" different, we need to continually reinforce a new message until it becomes our habit. Self-talk is a valuable asset in the change process. Ask yourself throughout the day, "How are we doing?" Perhaps at the end of the day, develop a habit of spending five to ten minutes almost debriefing with yourself on this question. Think of it as something like your antivirus software on your computer: replay your day and identify instances in which you really lived your new chosen coaching habits. Also, review those instances in which you had a "snap back" or fell back on an old habit.

6. **Select a partner**—Select someone with whom you have an existing trusting relationship. While you can be open to constructive feedback from any source, ask your partner to be particularly tuned into who you "are" in different experiences and let you know specifics. This is a terrific way to make some mid-course corrections or to identify triggers that may challenge your new way of being, e.g., a particular meeting or interacting with a specific person.

    Use the intentionality framework: Reframe...Reclaim... Rejoice...Re-choice.

7. **Sincerely ask for input, feedback, and help**—In both formal and informal ways, give those around you permission to help you through constructive feedback and input. Be brave and encourage others to speak up if they have ideas, see things differently, or are missing something from the relationship. This means that you risk being vulnerable, and opening yourself up. Take the risk, the payoff of stronger, trusting relationships is worth it.

Notes:

6 The Coach Leader Starter Kit

The Four Basic Behaviors of a Coach Leader

Do not wait; the time will never be "just right." Start where you stand, and work with whatever tools you may have at your command, and better tools will be found as you go along.
—Napoleon Hill

There are risks and costs to a program of action. But they are far less than the long-range risks and costs of comfortable inaction.
—John F. Kennedy

Now that we have begun the work of more consistently holding the coach leader model in our heads, hearts, and guts and applying that new way of being to ourselves first—coaching ourselves to our personal best, coaching others to lead from their seats, and being willing to be coached by others—the timing is finally right to identify and then practice the foundation behaviors on which the coaching model is built. Yes, this is the "doing" part. Are you ready?

One of my organizational clients quipped, as they were working to become coach leaders together, "this coaching starter kit is where touchy feely meets nuts and bolts." I couldn't have said it better myself. "Touchy feely" means to bring your emotions and your intuition to this discussion—lead with them—and blend in the logic, the "nuts and bolts," so that we can identify and then take step-by-step inspired action to become more skillful. It is a unique coupling of art and science, and that's what makes coaching such a powerful force for constructive, positive transformation.

This coaching starter kit also provides you with all the basic tools you need to start doing what a good coach leader does. And with these tools you can do a darn fine job of it too.

I also want to give a gentle but firm warning here. What you are about to read talks about communication; coaching is a very sophisticated, intentional way of interacting and because we interact primarily through communication, that is what gets privileged first. But don't dismiss what you read thinking that you have already mastered these skills. I know very smart and exceptionally good leaders who don't use these communication tools—simply because they don't know how!

I also want to remind everyone one more time that this entire book, the system that I have taught, refined (and yes, even argued with at times myself), is based on the legitimate and empowering assumption that we are all leaders in our organizations! Regardless of title, salary, position, or office location, you lead from your seat.

Repeat after me. My seat IS a power seat! Make that one of your mantras or affirmations each and every day if it is not there already.

Creating leaders at all levels is the key to being successful and happy as a workplace community. It is *the* key! And what I am about to share with you is the way any organization, working together at all levels, can create those leaders around us.

At this point in our work together, some of you may be saying to yourself, "well I'm just a _____ (fill in the blank with your current job title; for example, first shift cook in the kitchen or senior analyst or whatever)." You think "no one reports to me so there really isn't anyone that I can coach other than me."

I believe that this is stinkin' thinkin' some of that same-old, same-old thinking that has us stuck in our current habits. I am encouraging you to try this different perspective on for size: I can and should coach all day and every day to everyone with whom I interact. *That means that I coach myself, my teammates, my boss, others in my organization, and even those who are my clients, customers, or patients. In fact, if I choose to expand my thinking even further, I can and should coach my family, friends, and community. I can and should coach because it feels good to me and to others; it has the potential to bring out the best in others and it positions my organization and my community for maximum positive results. I am a coach leader. It is my way of being, rather than an intervention. In fact, it has become such a part of who I am, that I never have to say the words, "let me coach you."*

To continue to collect and then connect our learning from earlier chapters, remember that *coaching* happens in everyday, intentional conversations. They aren't something you set aside to do at some point in the day. They are "moments of truth" or "just in time coaching moments" when the spirit of coaching shines through. Don't underestimate or undervalue the impact that these exchanges have. And just to give you a taste of what I mean, here are some sample phrases that are characteristic of full-throttle engagement and coaching conversations:

- I have an idea for how to tackle this problem.
- What do you think?
- That solution might work. I would have never come up with that. It's not what we've done in the past but it might be even better. Let's give it a try.
- You look swamped, how can I help?
- Awesome job!
- Got it—_____ (then saying nothing, listening instead).
- Conversely, here are some sample phrases you should never hear in coaching conversations

- That's not in my job description.
- Only the manager makes decisions.
- I can't do anything without checking in with her first.
- That will never work here.
- Nothing ever changes around here.
- It's my way or the highway.
- I will now coach you (coach leaders never say they are coaching, because they are always coaching!).
- Who does he think he is, offering solutions and taking the lead, he's not our boss. What a suck up!

See the difference? The coaching phrases are simply ways to promote productive conversation. The others, those you never hear in a coaching conversation, are designed to shut someone down. Which would you prefer?

Starter Kit Directions

Coaching is high-quality collaborative inquiry. It is far more about asking questions so as to assist those around you with whom you are in community, to help them find their own answers, options, and solutions to their challenges and opportunities.

These are the foundational coaching skills that, when practiced faithfully day-in-and-day-out, are guaranteed to allow you to lead from your seat; improve your relationships; allow you to have a more fulfilling, satisfying work experience; and ultimately result to better service to your customers/clients/patients and overall success. They include:

- **Coach Leader Behavior #1:** Understand and positively exploit the signature strengths of your communication style and the communication style of others.
- **Coach Leader Behavior #2:** Faithfully practice engaged, clear listening.
- **Coach Leader Behavior #3:** Choose words with great care (intentional languaging).
- **Coach Leader Behavior #4:** Be aware of my nonverbal communication and make sensible choices that help (intentional

nonverbal communication).

Go back to Chapter 5 and take a look at the dialogue principles (authenticity, inclusion, respect, thoughtfulness, and openness). Wouldn't you agree that the coach leader behaviors are elegantly woven into these four behaviors?

The initial step in activating these foundational coaching behaviors as your new leadership habit (your way of being in the organization) is to adopt a ritual of intentionally calling forth the coach in you several times each day. At the beginning and end of each day, and before major segments of your day (for example, an important meeting, an interview, a talk with a colleague, etc.), simply spend a few moments doing the following:

- **Declare your intention**—First to yourself and then out loud to others, say it in an affirmative, first person declarative sentence(s). Use your own words but be sure that you are capturing the essences of coaching. For example, "Today, I choose to make a difference in all of my interactions. I see others' signature strengths. I appreciate my organization and my colleagues. I choose to coach, to think the best of a person or situation. I choose a framework of positivity and possibility." You might even think about a sentence or two that will assist you in staying in the moment and focus on embedding your new habit. Jot them down in the margins in a journal or notebook so you can look at them and refine them as you get better and better at this new method of interacting.

- **See others as "perfect enough"**—This is a huge and dramatic shift for some of us. Let go of past and present judgments, organizational rap sheets, and the need to fix people and simply see them as "perfect enough." They are where they are supposed to be in their own evolutionary journey. They are capable and well-intended. They are our colleagues. Think the best. Expect the best. Give the best of yourself, regardless of what is going on around you. This isn't an excuse to settle for good. Moving from good to great is a part of becoming the best that we can be. So keep moving. At the same time, recognize that it is a process and each stage serves a purpose in our life. Don't be hyper critical or grossly impatient with ourselves or others as we grow and learn.

- **Take full advantage of the moment**—Remember that our point of power is in the present moment. What you do and say matters. We cannot change the past. Nor does it always predict the future. We are not yet living in the future. But what we choose to be and do in *this* moment will shape what happens next. In whatever you are doing, live in the moment. Bring the best of you to bear on the situation. Come off autopilot and be intentional. The results will amaze and delight you.
- **Maintain a heightened level of awareness**—Same-old, same-old thinking and behaving can be intoxicating. Beware of dysfunctional comfort in yourself. Choose to be in the moment.

From this place of readiness and choicefulness, we are well positioned to examine each of the foundational coaching behaviors and begin to incorporate them into our everyday practices. A big part of being a coach leader and leading from your seat is doing more than expected; never settling for doing an average or "good" job. To really wring the most value from this learning we need to both understand each behavior and then practically apply that new understanding in our work lives. We've got to connect the dots between each foundational behavior and how it can help you be a leader from your seat.

To jumpstart that process, each tool given in both the starter kit and in the advanced coach-leader behaviors includes a detailed description of each behavior followed by a story, situation, or example intended to help each of you to better understand how this tool can help you to lead from your seat. These practical illustrations of the behaviors in action answer the question "Now what?" Now that I understand this new behavior, what do I do differently to put it into action and lead from my seat?

It's also key to discover your own personal method or rhythm for acquiring these new behavior habits and for breaking or dialing back the old ones. One of the very best ways to dislodge old habits and replace them with new ones is the intentional method outlined in Benjamin Franklin's *Autobiography*. It's simple, effective, and worth considering.

Franklin identified thirteen key behaviors (he called them virtues) that he wanted to own, to grow within himself. He created a basic chart in his journal that allowed him to track his progress of integrating new habits into his everyday behavior. He gave his full and undivided attention to *one habit each week*. In this way, he hoped to intentionally gain mastery over that one new habit and then shift his focus to the next new behavior.[25]

I think there is marvelous wisdom in Franklin's approach. I have used something similar myself with great results. Try it. For one week, practice using one new coach leader behavior routinely throughout your day. Coach yourself on that one skill only. At the end of the day, think/write about how you well you did. I've always advocated the one-thing-at-a-time approach. But if that doesn't work for you, find a way that works even better. However, do keep in mind that writing about your experience with these new coach leader behaviors is important to your overall success in keeping them alive in your work life.

And just a note on set up. Because each of these tools in the tool kit are meaty, I have set them up as if they were their own chapter. Read them as such. Absorb each behavior. Try it out even before you move into the next because what follows is a lot of information and I want you to be able to understand it first and then internalize it so that you can start using it effectively.

Your journey into the realm of the coach leader is about to begin. As the Italians say, *buono fortuna*, which literally means good fortune. I wish you all the fortune a well-honed organization running on full throttle can bring you.

Vroom, vroom. Ladies and Gentlemen, start your engines please...

Coach Leader Behavior #1:

Understanding and Positively Exploiting Your Own Communication Style and the Communication Style of Others

Great coach leaders are thoughtful, effective communicators. That, at a minimum, means that they willingly engage in ongoing communication loops or exchanges, in which they:

— get their message across in a way that the other person(s) can hear it, let it in, and then do something with it.

and

— are open to receiving a message in the same spirit of community and collaboration.

An important initial step in realizing your full potential as an effective communicator is to recognize and understand your own communication style at work, as well as the styles of your colleagues and others in your workplace experience. This awareness can make all the difference in the world. It can be the "aha!" moment for you!

By coming to this new level of understanding, you can begin to choose approaches, words, tone, and body language that help you to both get your message across and, at the same time, truly "get" the message that the other person is sharing. There is no right or wrong style; rather, each has its signature strengths, i.e., elements that help us to be effective communicators, as well as its shadow side, or the characteristics of a style that can derail us or get in our way.

To facilitate this learning, I am offering you a simple communication style assessment tool. If you aren't clear on what your dominant style is, it is vitally important that you take the assessment before moving forward. This will allow the other tips, tools, and techniques to have greater meaning for you and, in my experience, you will be better situated to successfully implement new behaviors into your daily routine. I also encourage you to share this assessment tool with teammates and colleagues. In so doing, you will learn about the styles of others around you and it can stimulate some great discussion at team meetings on how to do a better job of communication. Take the assessment and reflect on the results now![26]

Communication Style Self-Assessment

Instructions: Read each pair of behavioral characteristics below and place a check on the line after the word in each pair that best describes you. Please focus on you in the workplace today, not how you would like to be in the future. Remember to tell yourself the unvarnished truth as there is NO right or wrong answer. Then add up the number of times you placed a check after a word in column A.

	A		B	
Animated	_____	or	Passive	_____
Take charge	_____	or	Go along with group	_____
Assertive	_____	or	Hesitant	_____
Demanding	_____	or	Accepting	_____
Emotional	_____	or	Reserved	_____
Confronting	_____	or	Supportive	_____
Talkative	_____	or	Quiet	_____
Bold	_____	or	Timid	_____
Intense	_____	or	Subdued	_____
Direct	_____	or	Indirect	_____
Your Total	_____		Do not total	XXXXXX

Circle the number on the horizontal (going across) line in the graph below that corresponds with your score for column A. This score measures the level of assertiveness in your communications. You will now do the same for the word pairs below. You will add the total for D not C. Then, circle the number on the vertical (going up and down) line corresponding to your D score. This score measures your orientation to people versus tasks.

Now, connect the two circled numbers with a line. For most of us, that line will be located in one of the four quadrants, each representing a distinct communication style. This is, most likely, your dominant way of communicating.

Now, look through the following few pages and read the description of that style thoroughly.

You should identify with about 75 – 80 percent of the characteristics listed for your style. Reflect on this information. Does it fit? Please understand that each of us, depending on the situation, could find ourselves using any of the four styles. However, we are interested in better understanding our dominant style.

If, when connecting your two scores, you drew a line directly on the border between two styles, then you may have dominant aspects of both. I ask that you consider each of those when determining your dominant style. Does one or the other feel like a better fit?

Finally, in rare instances, a person will find themselves at the intersection of all four styles—this happens when both scores are five. If you find yourself in that situation, please return to the two sets of paired words to be sure that your responses truly represent your communication pattern at work now. If that is the case, then carefully review the characteristics of all four styles and determine which one (or potentially two) feels as though it is the best fit for you.

	C			D
Flamboyant	_____	or	Restrained	_____
Spontaneous	_____	or	Planned	_____
Responsive	_____	or	Detached	_____
Impulsive	_____	or	Methodological	_____
Sociable	_____	or	Aloof	_____
Sentimental	_____	or	Analytical	_____
People-oriented	_____	or	Task-oriented	_____
Outgoing	_____	or	Reserved	_____
Dramatic	_____	or	Self-controlled	_____
Friendly	_____	or	Unfriendly	_____
Do not total	XXXXXX		Your Total	_____

Understanding Communication Styles

As I said earlier in this conversation, each style has brilliances and, at the same time, shadow sides to it. Simply being aware of your style can help you to be a more effective communicator. Understanding that everyone does not have that same style is equally important. Because each style adds unique value to a team or an organization, I would never want you or anyone else to attempt to become someone that you are not. You are pretty terrific just the way that you are. For example, a Commander does not need to aspire to becoming an Analyzer. Having said that, armed with the more information about our own style as well as the communication style others, we can refine or make modest adjustments in the way that we share our message and receive messages from others. Using this new knowledge intentionally will open the door for us to more effectively participate in the life of our organizations! You may be surprised at how differently things will flow.

TAKE THE LEAD

FOCUS ON RELATIONSHIPS

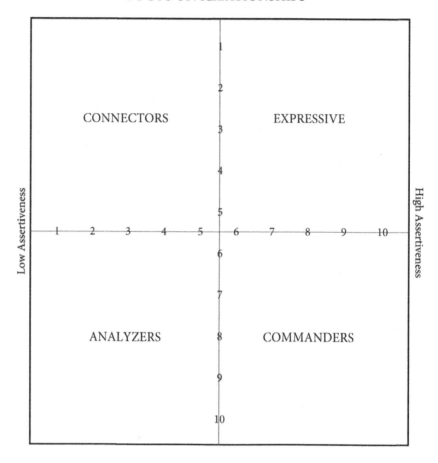

The following are summary descriptions of each communication style:

The Expressive

Prefers a direct, people-driven approach to communication. These communicators are generally assertive in their style and focused on building and enriching relationships in the workplace. They lead through emotional intelligence.

Characteristics

High energy

Exciting and fast paced

Receptive to new ideas

Expresses opinions openly and honestly

Likes involvement with others

Makes decisions rapidly

Aware of others and their feelings

Spontaneous

Imaginative

Competitive

Likes rapidly moving tasks and situations

Does not let the grass grow under their feet

Social

Disorganized

Daydreams

Easily bored with routine

Impatient with slow movers

The Connector

Prefers the indirect, people-driven approach to communication. Similar to the Expressives, these communicators thrive on developing and maintaining strong relationship bonds. However, they are generally less assertive than Expressives. They lead from their emotional intelligence as well as their intuition.

Characteristics

Warm and likable

Good listener

Eager to please

Cooperative and easy going

Able to see all sides

Loyal

Rarely tries to manipulate others

Highly intuitive and empathetic

Gets along with most people

Great team player

Nice to work with and work for

Provides a nurturing environment

Can be a pushover

Avoids conflict

Unable to say no

Very quiet at times

Values feelings over facts

The Commander

Prefers a direct approach, driven to task completion. These communicators are assertive and focused more on getting things done than on developing relationships. They lead primarily through logic.

Characteristics

Active and independent

Self-confident

Ambitious

Responds well to challenges

Needs personal success

Task-oriented

Sets high personal standards

Natural leader

Gets things done

Goal-oriented

Driven

Opinionated

Not a great listener

Gets bored when things slow down

Has difficulty being a follower

The Analyzer

Prefers an indirect idea and task-driven approach to communication. These communicators share a task orientation with the Commanders. However, they are less assertive. They too lead with their logic.

Characteristics

Good problem solver

Steady in approach

Logical

Deliberate

Intelligent and knowledgeable

Orderly, systematic, and methodological

Unassuming, calm, and stable

Efficient, hard worker

Takes work and responsibility seriously

Consistent and traditional

Likes clarity

Wants specifics

Needs all the facts

May become paralyzed

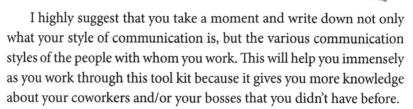

I highly suggest that you take a moment and write down not only what your style of communication is, but the various communication styles of the people with whom you work. This will help you immensely as you work through this tool kit because it gives you more knowledge about your coworkers and/or your bosses that you didn't have before.

Knowledge is power if used strategically. Now that we have new or reinforced insights into our communication style, we can become more aware and then more choiceful about who we show up as in interactions and how we communicate during those interactions. A heightened level of awareness is key to self-improvement. Do not become someone else. Do become your best self. Do more than expected as an effective communicator.

Now what? What can I do with my new understanding of the significance of communication styles that will make a difference at work and help me to lead from my seat?

Be intentional in your conversations and be aware of your own style and how different it may be from others. Be more mindful of the fact that the way you receive someone else's comments may relate to differences in style and vice versa. How someone else receives your message often relates to stylistic differences. Take this new knowledge into account to get your message across in a way that the other person can hear it, let it in, and take action. Choose to think the best of a person rather than the worst. Here's an example of how being aware of potential communication style differences can foster better relationships at work:

You are convinced that your boss really doesn't like you much or value your opinion. When you are with her, she seems "all business." She rarely asks about you or your family or what's going on in your life. She wants to get down to it right away. She interrupts you when you are giving her the background on an issue and asks you to get to the point. And she is all about getting the task done. It feels like impatience to you. And it doesn't feel as though she is listening to what you have to say. Your feelings are sometimes bruised and you have been avoiding conversations with her lately.

Armed with the new knowledge that you have a "connector" communication style, it is important to remember that you love the story behind the situation. And that you really appreciate personal connection as a part of communication. From your learning, you might suspect that your boss has a commander style. That doesn't make her bad or wrong—just different. It may have nothing to do with whether she likes you or not. Taking that into account, you could choose to shorten your background piece, write it down, and give it to her ahead of time and be specific about the help that you need from her to move forward. Instead of avoiding conversations with her, you can specifically ask if she has time to listen to you and think through a situation. You could choose to talk to her about different styles, share the assessment with her, and then discuss how to communicate more effectively with one another. Meet her half-way. Think the best rather than rush to judge negatively or imagine the worst. Be the best communicator that you can be. This is you leading from your seat! Size up the situation from an adult perspective and keep the overall good and the welfare of your boss in mind. Be creative. Shake up same-old, same-old patterns. Remember, you are only in charge of you! You cannot change your boss. She is in charge of changing her behavior (or not).

Now it's your turn! Describe a situation or relationship that could benefit from a new appreciation of communication style differences. Identify some specific actions that you can take to improve things and demonstrate your leadership. If you want, take the space at the end of this chapter to write down what you're thinking. Or write it down in a notebook or journal. Commitments seem to stick better when you actually write them, and you are making commitments to yourself about learning how to be a good coach by thinking of specific actions you can do.

Coach Leader Behavior #2:

Faithfully Practice Engaged, Clear Listening

Now that you have a fresh perspective on how people communicate, we can turn to the opposite end of the spectrum: listening. There is no better gift that we could bestow on our colleagues, teammates, clients, and our organizations than to become a more engaged, clear listener. In fact, there is no more impactful gift that we can give ourselves.

Listening is the very essence, the soul, of coach leadership. It has the potential in and of itself to be transformative because it provides us an ideal chance to learn and discover. Through engaged, clear listening, we get to send our curiosity on a mission.

Fully engaged listening means bringing the full monty of yourself to an exchange. You are present in the moment, undistracted, and attentive. Clear listening means that we are open and curious about learning and absorbing everything from the dialogue. It doesn't assume that we must immediately analyze or judge what we're hearing. Engaged, clear listening can yield disproportionate results when compared to the effort involved. You will be so much wiser, connected, and alive; so much more aware and attuned to the people and the environment around you.

Shakespeare dares us in King Lear to, "Look with thine ears." Research supports the power of engaged, clear listening. Study after study affirms that 9 out of 10 (90 percent) employee problems stem from someone not feeling heard!

Despite all of this evidence, listening is still rarely taught at any educational level. It relies primarily on emotional and intuitive intelligence and, for this reason, has often been undervalued in the Industrial and even in the Information Ages' organizational and leadership models.

In those eras, we required professionals to have strong writing skills. Excellent oral communication skills were emphasized and highly sought after. Today listening is fast becoming a value-added strength in business. Get ready for it. Tom Peters believes that the "single most strategic strength that an organization can cultivate, is a commitment to listening on the part of every member of the organization."[27] Check out the Coaching TO GO section for information on his brief video on the subject.

Do you consider yourself, today, at work, an extraordinary listener? When I ask audiences to think about that question and honestly answer it, only a handful has a strong conviction that they possess above-average skill in this area. Even fewer have made it a priority to take an educational program focused entirely on listening. And I must acknowledge that this level of listening is more challenging for some communication styles; it does not come as naturally to some as others. If we are to become coach leaders and assist ourselves, our colleagues, and our organizations to be the best that we/they can be, then we must resolve to consistently be an extraordinary listener. In my opinion, there is nothing else that you can do that will advantage your team more than practicing engaged, clear listening.

Let's connect our heart, head, and gut and embrace this learning with gusto. I want to share my seven secrets to listening with a coach leader's ear. I will promise you that if you wholeheartedly make these your habits, your experiences will be transformed over time!

Developing a coach leader's ear

1. Practice silence—The first and most potent step toward more engaged listening is to practice silence regularly. There are two aspects of silence that deserve our attention. First, in order to make room to listen, we must quiet all of the thoughts that are competing for our mind's attention. On average, Americans have about sixty-thousand thoughts each day; most are what is generally considered negative and repetitive.[28]

Because listening is an inspired action, we need to focus our attention on the listening instead of sharing our attention with many, many thoughts and also attempting to listen. Now, I know that many of us have become avid multitaskers. Here is an important question: is multitasking the most effective way of getting things done effectively at work? The answer is no. In fact, studies have shown that we lose ten IQ points when we are attempting to multitask (we do get them back when we stop!). And recent studies have suggested that it is impossible to actually multitask. This begs the question, why try?

Yes, I know that we can do basic functions such as walking and talking at the same time. But when it comes to developing and tending to relationships and being a part of workplace conversations, I am encouraging you to "single handle" the act of listening. This means to pay undivided attention to the other person(s). Quiet your "head trash," all of those other thoughts flying through your mind. Gently, easily do your best to just listen. Do not mentally argue with the speaker. Do not create your grocery list in your head, while appearing as though you are listening. Do not wait your turn to talk. Listen instead. There is so much to discover through active, engaged listening. Mine it for every insight that is available. Listen for the words that are used; the tone of the speaker's voice; the facial expression and body language (if present with the person); and, even listen for what is not said. There is great value to be had there.

Second, silence can be a useful tool for a coach leader. It offers the other person(s) the opportunity to consider, reflect, and then access their own insights and answers to options and challenges. Remember, depending on a person's communication style, time to think through something and create a response is very constructive. Listening presents us all with an opportunity to take style into account to become a more effective communicator.

2. Tune In—Engaged, clear listening requires that we not simply hear, but rather listen at a deeper level. In my own experience, observing hundreds of professionals and thousands of conversations in the workplace, I believe that many of us have, for a variety of reasons, developed a habit of superficial listening. We may think that we already know what the other person is going to say. We may have already decided on "the answer" and listening becomes nothing more than waiting our turn to

manage or direct. Or we may be preoccupied and have not created the space to listen that we discussed above. As coaches, we are called on to tune in to our colleagues. Be interested rather than interesting. Suspend judgments; you really do not know what the other person is going to say. If you are physically present with the other person(s), face her; gently look her in the eyes. Invite the person to sit with you, if possible, with nothing separating you (sit on the same side of the desk or table). This does not mean that we need to invade someone's personal space. Allow the standard three to five feet between the two of you.

3. Reflect Back—From time to time in the course of a conversation, simply choose to let the other person know that you are engaged with them by telling them, in your own words, what you have heard so far. Do this when there is a natural lull in the conversation. Do not present your understanding as though it is fact. Simply present it as what you have heard so far and ask if you have it right. For example, "It sounds as though you…do I have that right?" Or, "Let me see if I'm hearing you correctly so far…" It is important to use your own words and not parrot back what the person just said.

4. Constructively Label—At times, as you reflect back what you have heard, it may be useful to offer a label for the feelings or thoughts that you are hearing. This is not done in a "know-it-all" way; rather, it is best offered as part of a question with the intention of helping the speaker to gain some insight and potentially take some action. For example, "It sounds to me from what you are describing that you feel really overwhelmed right now? Is that true?" If it is, then you can follow up by asking the person to identify one thing that they can do to feel just a little less overwhelmed. If not, then ask them to label their feelings more accurately.

5. Clarify—Sometimes, it is best to just admit that you aren't quite sure what the point is that the other person(s) is making. Something such as, "I'm not sure that I understand. Try to explain it in a different way so that I get it" can be helpful.

6. Acknowledge—Let the person know that you are fully engaged and tracking along with them in a conversation using either a verbal or nonverbal acknowledgement or prompt. The best known nonverbal prompt is a slight nodding of the head. A verbal prompt can also be useful and is the only way to get this job done when you are not physically with the other person. I often say, "Tell me more..." to encourage the speaker and let them know that I am engaged and interested. A simple *ummm humm* will do perfectly. Send consistent messages that you are really in the conversation with them, but don't overdo it.

7. **Summarize**—Finally, unless the conversation is a very short hallway exchange, it is critical to summarize your understanding of the outcome of your discussion. It continues to surprise me that four people leaving a business meeting can genuinely have four completely different understandings of the outcome. Take a minute or two to confirm your take on the conversation to be sure that your understanding is shared by the other person. A short written follow-up can also be helpful. Check in on your intention if you write a brief follow-up. Is it to be an effective communicator and contribute to a successful outcome? Or is it more about protecting yourself (CYA—covering your own a_ _)?

Intentional Listening

Master these secrets and you will be well on your way to becoming a great listener, with all of the benefits that we have already discussed. At the end of this chapter, you will find some simple exercises and other resources to reinforce these secrets. And while these secrets are a powerful place to begin this work, they cannot replace a full learning program on listening. I dare you to make the commitment to take such a course. Many of my clients' organizations have a course on listening as part of their internal professional development curriculum. Check out your organization's course offerings.

When you have achieved greater command over the basics of engaged, clear listening, you will be well positioned to further advance your skills and ability by more intentionally listening for clues that can help you to be a better coach leader to your colleagues, your boss, and others in the workplace. If you are ready, begin to actively listen for:

- Habits that may tell you where the other person is today in their thinking, feeling, and behaving.

- Habits that may tell you what is keeping this person "stuck" or what is getting in their way.
- Habits that may tell you something about how this person can move forward using their personal brilliances.

For example, a conversation may yield some insights into a person's current relationship with money. That may help you to understand their current determination to save a certain amount of money from their salary.

If a person consistently talks about how bad things are and portrays the sky as "always falling," they may be holding themselves back because of fear or scarcity thinking. Finally, when someone tells you that when the going gets tough, he gets going, you may find that determination is a strength for this person and is a characteristic that has helped him to move beyond obstacles in the past.

When you are ready to graduate to intentional listening, begin to pay attention to the clues. Every conversation is rich with such information. It is there for those of us who choose to listen for it. There is no better way to experience full engagement than through listening and being heard.

Now what? What can I do with my new understanding of engaged, clear listening that will make a difference at work and help me to lead from my seat?

Not feeling heard can be painful and debilitating. It can have the same effect of a burr under a saddle—a constant irritant that can infect a relationship or your team's dynamics. On the other hand, the simple act of genuinely listening to someone can help someone to grow, reach their full potential, and feel respected and worthy. Listening is the it factor in coach leadership. It's the crown jewel of engagement. It's that important. It comes more natively to some communication styles, but everyone can enhance their ability to listen by developing a new discipline in our everyday conversations. Here's a brief example that illustrates how we can apply active listening techniques to open up new avenues for creative solutions to tough problems and lead from our seats.

You and Sara have worked together as teammates for more than five years. She has an idea a minute and is quite talkative. You've developed a habit of tuning her out when she talks to you—maybe you pick up every third word—or multitasking during your conversations so that they aren't a total waste of time! Sometimes you feel a twinge of guilt for behaving this way—it is disrespectful and downright rude at times. Lately, Sara has really looked hurt following your brush off. On the other hand, you are busy and she is irritating, so maybe it's "justified." Everyone else seems to really like Sara and her friendly approach. But she really rubs you the wrong way.

Some tension has developed within your team around some mistakes that were made on a report and team members are pointing the finger at each other. Rather than run to your boss to solve the growing problem, you are willing to lead from your seat and work to resolve this and stop the bad behavior before it gets any worse. Sara really might be able to help. You decide to intentionally set aside your past perceptions, choosing to see her through a different lens and ask for her assistance, support, and advice on this thorny issue. The two of you may be able to sit down with the other team members and get things ironed out and moving in the right direction.

This time, when you talk to Sara, you sit next to her, put aside your other work, look directly at her and give her your full attention. You choose not to interrupt, to take notes on what she has to say without quickly judging her remarks, and give her your undivided attention. You reflect back what you heard when she was finished. You clarify a few points. One of her ideas strikes you as simple, do-able and low risk. And it just might get the job done. Your teammates love food! Sara suggests that the whole team order a special lunch and plan to talk about the issue together. She even had two good ideas on how to frame the conversation so that it would be constructive. You both agree to work on this together. Sara leaves the conversation feeling upbeat rather than beaten up and there is a spark of possibility around resolution.

PS. You learned that your perception of Sara was off-base. She was worth listening to. You left the conversation feeling positive as well.

That's it. Seems small, doesn't it? Simple. Such changes can't possibly make a difference, right? Wrong. This is exactly what leading from your seat is all about. Taking the lead and changing your workplace one conversation, one relationship at a time. It can be really challenging to actively listen when you are rushed or the situation is charged and stressful. Start somewhere, anywhere today to develop a new listening habit and work your way up to difficult moments. Take action! Take the lead.

Coach Leader Behavior #3:

Intentional Languaging—Choose Words with Great Care

While engaged, clear listening is a powerful force in being a coach leader, it is one of four complementary elements of our coaching starter kit. In addition to great listening and positively exploiting knowledge of communication styles, intentional languaging is key to communicating effectively. Gently sharing what you hear in a caring and courageous way using the skills I'm about to introduce you to is what separates the good from the great in organizations

Bear in mind that when we are physically with someone, 93 percent of the message will come from something other than the words. Facial expression, eye movement, tone of voice, posture, etc. But that seven percent that comes from the words we choose can make the difference in the outcome of a conversation. And the words have an even greater impact when we are not with the other person, for example, when we are on the telephone.

As you now know, one of my personal mantras is, "big doors swing on small hinges." This reminds me that the little stuff matters. That sometimes it is the small, subtle things that make the difference. This is particularly true when it comes to having real, effective conversations at work. To become more choiceful with our words, we need to first become aware of a powerful duo in the language of coaching: micro-affirmations and micro-inequities. Together, they are called micro-messages.

The ground-breaking research on micro-messages was completed as part of the review and analysis of the efficacy of the Affirmative Action policies born in the 1960s and 1970s. Their impact at work has been

135

studied in broader ways since that time; and that additional research has consistently confirmed their significant impact.

Micro-affirmations are small, subtle acknowledgements. They are a way that we consciously and sub-consciously value others and, in this way, they form the cement of successful colleagueships and most caring relationships in and outside of our workplace communities. They have been proven to lead to greater measures of self-esteem and improved performance.

If, every time you walk into my cubicle, I look up and smile, that is a micro affirmation.

When I simply say, thanks, job well done, that is a micro-affirmation.

Micro-inequities are equally subtle behaviors that devalue people. Again, while they are often semi– or subconscious, they act to consistently "wall the person out." Sometimes, they are under the organizational radar screen and it can be challenging to uncover them completely.

If I, not once or twice, but regularly leave your name off the email list of my inner circle of colleagues, that is a micro-inequity.

If I regularly ask others' opinions at meetings but routinely skip you, that is a micro-inequity.

Remember, one of the ways of being a coach leader is to come off autopilot and be aware and be purposeful or choiceful about our thoughts, feelings, and behaviors. Intentional languaging is yet another critical application of this way of being. For us, there is no legitimate reason for continuing to engage in micro-inequities. We choose. We are not simply a product of our habits. We must become aware and then decide who we show up as in our conversations and relationships and how effectively and affirmatively we will communicate.

This chapter is packed with tips, tools, and techniques to breathe life into these skills and make them your own, taking into account your unique style and brilliances. But you are the only person who can flip the on switch and activate them in your life and sustain them as your new dominant habits.

From this place of renewed awareness, I want to emphasize seven basic elements of intentional languaging. They are deceptively simple, but not easy to do day in and day out. As you master these, and they become habit instead of effort, you will take yet another step closer to being your best self at work and leading from your seat.

Choosing your words becomes even more powerful when coupled with active listening. Imagine, for a moment, that you are in a conversation with someone who is obviously and genuinely listening to your every word. There are no interruptions, no judgments, no subtle put downs. In fact, there are small signals that affirm and acknowledge you. Now imagine that, after listening intently to you, the other person in this conversation responds with well-chosen words that allow you to feel heard, while at the same time are clear and crisp, help you to dig deep for your own answers, and challenge your same-old, same-old way of thinking.

Honestly, how would you feel at the end of that imaginary conversation? If you are being honest, I think that you will conclude that you would feel pretty darn good. Stronger. More capable. Listened to. Heard. Relieved. Back on track.

That's the reward. And we get to co-create just those kinds of conversations at work. And, after you have found your coach leader groove, these conversations feel really good. It's a win. You do your part. Let others do theirs.

Seven Elements of Intentional Languaging

1. **Being crisp and clear**—Take the time to be crisp and clear in your communications. Be straightforward *without being harsh or blunt.* For many reasons, it seems to me that we have developed the opposite habit—we seem to work hard at intentional ambiguity! Think about it. We sacrifice clarity to avoid potential litigation; to sidestep conflict; to pretend that we know what we are talking about; to prove just how educated we are; or to try not to hurt someone else's feelings. We expect that others will read (or hear) between the lines and we cross our fingers that they will get our disguised messages. Finally, we become indignant when they don't get the message, even though we have not done our part by being clear.

So, today begin to practice *clarity* by selecting the very best words for the situation and avoiding ambiguous words. Routinely begin to ask yourself: "Is this as clear as this message can be?" Also, avoid the use of superlatives unless they are essential for clarity. Every single situation cannot be a disaster! Routinely ask yourself for verification when you want to use a superlative: "Is it really true that he is NEVER on time?" "Does she ALWAYS yell when you ask a question?" There is a simple exercise at the end of the chapter to challenge you to get *clear* in your everyday conversations. Take the challenge!

2. **Applying the pronoun test**—Although they are some of the smallest words in our sentences, they send an important micromessage to the listener(s). Be intentional in their use. Use "I" when owning or describing your thoughts, feelings, perceptions, or opinions. Use "we" to share successes and team efforts and to emphasize partnerships, collaborations, and community. Be very aware of the tone of your voice when using the word "you."

   Of course, there is nothing wrong with the word "you" and it is frequently the clearest choice. Having said that, this word can land poorly with a blaming or accusatory tone of voice or a harsh choice of words. So, if you open up a conversation with something like, "I've been told that you're fighting with Mary, too!" you certainly aren't in the coaching space and it may feel as though you have reached a conclusion before hearing the listener's point of view. And adding the word "too" at the end would indicate that you think that this bad behavior is a pattern. An alternative might sound like, "I'm getting the sense that you and Mary disagree about the _____. Is that true? How did you two end up here? What is the plan to work through this?"

   Finally, who in the heck is "they"? When I ask team members who "they" are or "them" is when used in a sentence, the most frequent response is, you guessed it! "I don't know! The second most frequent response is, "you know, them, the executives!" Remember our commitment to clarity. If everyone involved in a conversation is clear on who "they" is, then use it. Otherwise, choose a different, crisper way to describe those involved.

3. **Languaging the Positive**—I want to begin by telling you what this does not mean. Languaging the positive does not mean that we put on rose-colored glasses and ignore personal or organizational challenges. That's the workplace equivalent to rearranging the deck chairs on the Titanic. It also does not mean that we become a team of Pollyannas, sacrificing authenticity for over-the-top hyper-optimism. Now that we have that out of the way, we can talk about how profound an impact a constructive approach can have on an individual, a team, or an entire organization. Great coach leaders know that there are plenty of opportunities to sincerely frame discussions in a positive or constructive way. They also realize the benefits that will almost immediately accrue to you and to those surrounding you when you choose to include positivity and possibility as part of your everyday leadership. Here is the short list of the benefits of routinely languaging the positive:

- Tap into innovation and creative problem solving more effectively.
- Predispose those around you to believe that things can "get right" and that they can play a role in making that happen.
- Reduce the time it typically takes to make mid-course corrections or manage/recover from a "crisis."
- Help to further establish a healthy workplace community.
- Engage in healthy, meaningful conflict.
- Learn more easily from challenges and failures.
- Set the stage to avoid making the same mistake in the future.
- Grow members of the team and unlock the best in everyone.
- Foster a safe environment in which accountability is consistently practiced.

Languaging the positive simply means that we choose the most positive and constructive words to fit the circumstances. In so doing, we become more effective communicators because, more often than not, we are getting our messages across in a way that the other person can hear them, let them in, and then do something with the information or knowledge. Yes, that's all there is to it! But remember, big doors swing on small hinges—little stuff makes a huge difference when done consistently.

There are some simple exercises to enhance your understanding of this concept at the end of the chapter. They focus on sentences and phrases that we could hear any day in a typical workplace. The challenge is to come off autopilot and really choose our words so that they are constructive. Give them a try on your own. Then use them to challenge your team.

4. **Describing Behavior Instead of Rushing to Judgment**—Some of my colleagues have shared with me that this element of intentional languaging—choosing to describe behavior rather than judge and label the behavior—is the most challenging new coaching skill to master and sustain. Why? I think that part of the explanation may be that we are all, in part, paid to and rewarded for making judgments! That's not a bad thing. But when it comes to behavior that is getting in someone's way, if we truly are committed to everyone's success, then we must use the most effective language to share our observations so that the person has the best chance of understanding and doing something about it.

It is clearer to describe a behavior than use a judgment that could well be misunderstood. For example, telling someone that they are not a "team player" is a vague judgment and it may be difficult for the person to know what to do differently to be a better team member. They may choose to feel misunderstood and resentful. These feelings, then, could give rise to other unproductive behaviors. If, on the other hand, we shared our observations by specifically describing a behavior (or an action) in a clear, charge neutral way, the other person has at least a better chance to get the picture we are portraying, have skillful discussion with us about it, and choose differently in the future. So, saying something like "Mary, in every team meeting for the past month, you have loudly disagreed with Steve on every point" gives the person a clear picture of what you have seen through your lens and what you have experienced. What happens next is engaged, clear listening and collaborative inquiry—otherwise known as coaching! Remember, you could be interpreting the situation incorrectly or you could be missing some key information. Talk before you pass judgment. Labels have an uncanny way of sticking with a person, even if they are inaccurate.

Don't miss the opportunity to practice this one! The exercises at the end of the chapter can be pretty tough.

5. **Practicing civility, respect, and consideration**—In ALL interactions, regardless of the message or the choices that others make, we are called upon as coach leaders to be civil, respectful, and considerate. And to practice what I preach, I want to be clear about what I mean by "civil." According to Professor PM Forni, "civility is an attitude of thoughtfully relating to others. It means that we must first be aware of others and then weave restraint, respect, and consideration into the very fabric of that awareness."[29]

This definition has a WOW-factor for me. I truly believe that if we all made civility a priority, we would be rewarded with a better world. While the subject of civility is a significant one for any coach leader, it is even more vital to the creation of workplace community, and for that reason merits a complete volume of its own in the *Everyday Leadership* Series. Look for it in the future. In practice, being civil, respectful, and considerate would mean that we do not engage in gossip in our organizations. It would require that we think the best of others until proven otherwise. Civility means that we don't interrupt someone. That we don't sacrifice the basics of "please and thank you" even when we are in a hurry. Most of us know, at some level, how to be civil. What we need to do now is to make it an everyday habit again!

6. **Telling the Story**—Storytelling is a right-brain activity. That makes it a strong match to the emerging organizational and leadership models that we learned about in Chapter 1. Many people in today's organizations want to know the details; they can handle the truth when it comes to financial data. But more than anything else, they want to be connected and inspired by a compelling story. Coach leaders understand this and make it their business to know how to communicate through story. They realize that the change process is better received and more easily sustained if everyone understands the story, the why behind the change. Although storytelling is more compatible with some communications styles, we all have the ability to add this to our communication repertoire. If this is not your current brilliance, check out some of the resources and suggestions in the Coaching TO GO section at the end of this chapter.

7. **"What If" Upping**—Rounding out the seven elements of intentional languaging is a quirky but valuable skill. I don't know about you, but when I was growing up professionally, we paid an awful lot of attention to thinking about, talking about, preparing for, and strategizing around the "worst case scenario"! This isn't necessarily a bad thing. We should consider different possible outcomes and how we will respond. But I believe that we may have gone overboard in our emphasis of the worst possible outcome. If we are going to play this "what if" game, then I believe that we owe it to ourselves and our organizations to be balanced and play it both ways. How about spending thinking about, talking about, dreaming about, and strategizing about the "best case scenario"? I call that "what if" upping (as opposed to the traditional what ifs that seem to spiral ever downward).

As a coach leader, it is so important that you develop a habit of expecting the very best and navigating the flow. It is equally important for each of us to encourage and cultivate that in others around us. Remember, from our discussion of intentionality that thoughts become things, so choose the good ones. What we think about does indeed help to shape our next reality. The skillful communicator keeps this in mind as s/he makes idea and word selections. What if everyone in your organization began to focus their energy and attention on working toward a shared, positive vision of the future? What if that turned out to be pretty amazing? What if all it took to begin this trend was for one person to do it? What if that one person is you?

Now what? What can I do with my new understanding of habitually choosing my words intentionally that will make a difference at work and help me to lead from my seat?

Being more conscious of your words and then making wise choices will help every single relationship or situation. It won't assure the outcome each time, but it will allow you to act as an adult, make a constructive contribution, control the things that you can, and become more influential. Intentional languaging can heal old wounds, be a time saver and help someone to feel better about herself. Some colleagues have asked if intentionally choosing your words isn't just being a little too PC (politically correct). Why can't we all just put on our big-girl and big-boy pants, they complain, and stop hanging on every word that is said.

I agree that we all must be adults and tell the truth as we see it. And we can all work on not taking every remark personally. Nevertheless, *how* we choose to message something will still be critically important to our level of success. Because this is about people, not machines. It is about creating community, not isolating one another. It is about engagement and that requires respect, consideration, and thoughtfulness. Intentional language is a huge WIN. It pays such big dividends once you get the rhythm of it. Make the effort. This is a terrific example of doing more than what is expected. You change you. And check out the results. Here are a few illustrations of the payoff of this work, how choosing your words with great care will allow you to lead from your seat:

You've been accused of taking more than your share of the credit for your team's achievements. It's true, your team has met every monthly sales goal for the entire year and your work is a major part of that success. And you're proud of that fact. In the past, faced with this type of feedback, you might have pouted for a while, chalked it up to others being jealous, ignored it altogether or gone straight to the boss's office to whine a little. Instead, as a coach leader, you choose not to become defensive or overreact. You consider the comments. You try to understand their meaning. Because you were so intentional, you learn that instead of using the pronoun "I" most of the time, it could be helpful to begin to use "we" more often to acknowledge that no one salesperson was responsible for hitting the goal. You find out that, coming from you, congratulating others on a job well done when closing a sale would mean a lot to the other team members. Small changes, big reward. The more you make these small shifts, the more you are seen as a leader.

Or consider this example:

Everyone in the department is chatting in the break room. Someone starts talking about the new guy and in an unfavorable tone of voice, announces that he is stuck up, not a team player, and won't last long. Other people pile on with their comments. "Yeah, he didn't come to the birthday party yesterday." "He just stays in his office and hardly talks to anyone!" Instead of engaging in this judgmental gossip, you intentionally take another approach. "Hey everyone, Mark is a pretty nice guy. I know him from softball and I think you're misjudging him. He is really shy until you get to know him. Then he's lots of fun. Give him a break." You make sure that your tone is neutral. Don't become a parent and scold everyone. This everyday choice is what leading from your seat means.

Finally, when a project is delegated to you with what seems to you to be vague directions and no sense of the final product, you talk to the person doing the delegating to be sure that you really understand the expectations. You actively listen, reflect back what you heard, clarify, frame it positively, and choose your words carefully when committing to tasks and time frames. Both of you walk away from the five minute exchange more certain that the project is on course and on time. Another way that each of us leads from our seat.

Coach Leader Behavior #4:

Intentional Nonverbal Messaging

I pointed out in the last coaching behavior that when you and I are together, 93 percent of the message comes from something other than the words! What a huge opportunity to become a more effective communicator—take responsibility for and control of your facial expressions, postures, gestures, eye positions, tone of voice, and the sounds that you make (sometimes called para-linguals).

When it comes to nonverbal mastery, there are two things to keep in mind:

1. Align nonverbals with your words to maximize your effectiveness. When there is an inconsistency between the message that your words send and the message of your eyes or your body, most people will choose to "get the message" through the nonverbal communication channel. So, if someone responds to a request with the word "fine" and at the same time uses eyes, facial expressions, and postures to send a message of annoyance, the person receiving the message will most often come away from the interaction believing that the person is annoyed.

    Whenever I talk about nonverbals with an audience or within a specific organization, someone almost always shares with me that they genuinely don't know that they are—for example, rolling their eyes during the meeting. If you really do not know, then your body is doing things behind your back—does that make sense? I have come to understand that what most people mean is that those eye movements are not intentional; they are a habit that we do not think about. It feels as though we don't know but we are the only ones in charge of our body and we are the ones who developed the habit in the first place. And the good news is that we are the only ones who can make a new choice!

Be intentional. Send the most effective message that you can with your words coupled with your actions. If you feel annoyed, then own the feeling. Express it with civility and be prepared to discuss a solution with your boss or your teammate. This is the mature behavior of a coach leader.

2. The other consideration when it comes to nonverbals is to avoid becoming hyper-correct. Sometimes a scratch of the nose simply means that it is allergy season and someone has an itchy nose. What we need to focus on is noticing patterns in ourselves and others. If they add to effective communications then keep doing them—they are contributing to your coach leadership. If they aren't then we need to surrender them in favor of something better. Have some fun with the list of the most common nonverbal cues found in the workplace. It is included in the Coaching TO GO section of this chapter. Remember, don't over-read signs in yourself or others.

Now what? What can I do with my new understanding of habitually choosing my nonverbal messages intentionally that will make a difference at work and help me to lead from my seat?

Sounds tell stories. Don't underestimate the power of nonverbal communications. They can be either micro-affirmations or micro-inequities. They give you the intentional opportunity to do good in small ways. I learned this lesson the hard way and I would like to share this embarrassing personal story with you so that you can avoid this mistake:

Over a decade ago, when my coaching enterprise, Vantage International, was brand new, I had a coaching conversation with one of my clients that turned out to be one of the most powerful learning moments in my career. Our coaching relationship was strong and the client used the time and space to achieve superior results. During one telephone conversation, the client mentioned in passing that he was a devotee of the game Dungeons and Dragons. My only response to this revelation was a slight drawing in of my breath, the way we do when we are surprised. It was very slight. The next question from my client was, "Don't you like people who play Dungeons and Dragons, Leta?"

Let's stop and think about this. A slight noise led my client to out a prejudice that I unconsciously held. He called me out. I had to admit my own filter, apologize, and be willing to talk about and think about this experience. For me, this was so revealing as to be one of those epiphany moments when my understanding and commitment to intentionality and to coaching deepened measurably. It also highlighted the mutual benefit that comes from the ebb and flow of coaching conversations. We learn, we teach, we listen, we ask questions, we support, we challenge, we lead, we follow—the elegant rhythm of engagement.

So there you have it, the four basic behaviors that are the heart and soul of coach leadership—the starter kit. So, get started! They are the very first steps of the doing part, and I truly believe that if everyone in your organization practiced these with determination, you would see a remarkable difference in the way people felt about their work. They would be engaged—and that is definitely a step in the right direction.

Coaching TO GO

The Coaching TO GO section is full of exercises, case studies, and other tips, tools, and techniques to make these starter skills come alive for you. So I have two questions for you: How good can you stand it? What are you willing to DO to promote full-throttle engagement?

1. **Must haves for your professional library**—There are two books that rise to the top when it comes to creating a coaching starter kit. The first is *Crucial Conversations* by Kerry Patterson and others. This is a practical guide with lots of suggestions for improving your intentional languaging. The second is the very best reference on civility that I have yet to find and read. It is *Choosing Civility: The 25 Rules of Considerate Conduct* by PM Forni. This is a small book that has a huge impact. Many of my clients are using it as part of their roadmap for cultural change.

2. **Check out the article**—Want more on engaged, clear listening? Check out the brief Power Point program on the Vantage

website on *clear listening*. It makes some very interesting points and reinforces this chapter's learning on the topic.

3. **Storytelling**—While you are checking out the Vantage website, why not read the article on "The Lost Art of Storytelling." Unleash the story teller in you!

4. **Fun listening exercise**—Here is a very simple and very brief exercise that you can do with your team to highlight the skills of active listening. Ask the coordinator of your team or staff meeting for ten minutes to conduct and debrief this exercise:

    a. Have your teammates move their chairs so that they are sitting back to back with a partner.

    b. For purposes of the exercise, ask one person to be the listener and one to be the talker. Give them just a quick moment to select their role.

    c. The listener will need to have pen/pencil and paper in front of them. And this is critical—they may not talk during the brief exercise!

    d. Now, tell the group that this is a very short exercise lasting only one-and-a-half minutes and that you will time them.

    e. Then, quickly ask the talker to describe in detail the front of their home or apartment and ask the listener to DRAW what they hear.

    f. After one-and-a-half minutes, call time and ask the talker to look over their partners shoulder to see the drawing.

This simple exercise creates some good opportunity for learning. First, ask the team for the communication barriers that you established: can't look at each other; can't ask questions; felt as though they had to hurry (although in reality almost everyone can thoroughly describe the front of their house in ninety seconds—we simply created the urgency!); it was very noisy because everyone was talking; and one person had to picture something in their minds and then describe it while their partner had to listen, and then translate the words to pictures (in other words move it from the left brain to the right brain).

WOW, all in one itty bitty exercise. Ask everyone what they learned. The talker had to be very specific and sequence their comments so that the other person could follow along and draw it correctly. The listener had to really dedicate themselves to simply listening. And for me, the biggest take away of all is that most of us want to look over the shoulder of our partner and see a picture that somehow looked like our house. In other words, we wanted our partner to "get it" and be successful in this exercise. **If we were to simply bring that level of desire to each of our conversations—genuinely wanting to do what we can to help the other person to "get our message"—then our workplaces would be better places to be.** Try it!

5. **Case Study**—Here is a simple case study to challenge your learning on these foundation skills. If the details of the case study don't seem relevant to your workplace, then create one that does. Use it as another exercise in your team or staff meeting.

A member of your team is playing a supporting role in a major project. He/she has just come back from a meeting that included higher level coworkers from within the office and staff from other offices and vendors. The employee is very frustrated because no decisions were made during the meeting. It wasn't apparent to the employee that any of his/her coworkers were taking the responsibility to make the decisions that needed to be made in order to move the project forward. How would you listen effectively? How would you choose to BE in the situation? What question could you ask to help the person think through their situation in a constructive way? What wouldn't you say or do?

6. **Tom Peters on Listening**—Check out a brief video by Tom Peters on the power of engaged, clear listening. Trust me, it will make you stop and think. It can be found in various places on the internet, including Tom's official website and on YouTube.

Then answer the question, "Am I an eighteen-second person?"

7. **Intentional Language Challenge**—Work your intentional languaging muscles using these simple exercises found on the Vantage website: www.vantage-inter.com. They use examples from everyday conversations that could be heard in your organization. Increase their value by working through them with teammates or as part of an in-service program.

8. **Body Language Quiz**—Challenge your knowledge of the meaning of these common workplace postures or gestures. The answers are found on the Vantage website: www.vantage-inter.com.

   What is the intended message for each of the following?

   - Leaning head or body forward
   - Steepling fingers
   - Crossing arms across chest
   - Rubbing or touching nose
   - Lowering head
   - Shifting away from person speaking
   - Blinking or clearing throat repeatedly
   - Putting hands over mouth
   - Rubbing back of neck
   - Crossed legs, foot moving in slight kicking motion
   - Chin in palm of hand with index finger extended alongside of cheek
   - Taking glasses on and off
   - Tugging ear
   - Sitting with ankles locked and fists clenched
   - Holding head in palm of hand

Notes:

Building Coach Leader Strength and Confidence:

Six More Advanced Coaching Behaviors

The best teacher is one who questions and suggests rather than directs, and inspires her listener with the wish to teach himself.
—**Edward Bulwer-Lytton**

By acquiring awareness, understanding, knowledge, and practice of the basic elements set forth in the starter kit in the last chapter, we are well positioned to live further into our best selves and build our strength and confidence as a coach leader. That means that we not only sustain our new habits of engaged, clear listening, intentional languaging, and intentional nonverbal messaging, but we actually expand beyond them through:

- Collaborative inquiry
- Truth seeking and truth telling
- Building others
- Growing others
- Goal setting and achievement

- Playfulness (the lighter side of coaching)

These are more advanced coach-leader skills, and with them you can build on the foundation you put in place with the four basic behaviors so that you can be confident, build on your strengths, and power your organization forward into the Conceptual Age with grace, humor, humility, and a healthy dose of certainty that all this right-brained thinking and acting really is the stuff of the future.

Please understand that we are dialing it up a notch here. The six skills presented in this chapter are more demanding to master and to sustain. Your commitment to being more intentional will pay huge dividends as you challenge yourself here. Just as we did with the basic behaviors, take them on one at a time. Do a "Ben Franklin." Practice one of these in a fanatically focused way each week. You will feel an energy gain as you add one skill after another to your leadership repertoire. A sense of power and freedom awaits you when you arrive at that stage of development in which you are using all of these behaviors in combination, day in and day out. Their interaction is potent.

Before we turn our attention to this next layer of learning and growing together, let's take a strategic pause to remind ourselves of the why. Why is becoming a coach leader so vital to your individual future, the future of your team and your organization, the future of the people who you serve, and the future of your community and our local, regional, national, and even international business communities? And yes, your action or inaction truly has consequences of this magnitude!

Here are the primary motivations for transforming yourself into a coach leader, regardless of your title, position, or salary:

Motivation #1—The traditional command and control organizational model and its companion, the authoritarian (parental) leadership approach, are no longer effective and are giving way to new ways of being together. In Authentic Conversations, the Showkeirs are brassy when they proclaim that, "Such systems have outlived their usefulness and are degrading to the human spirit."[30] I agree. We can choose to be part of the solution or part of the problem. Intentionally becoming a coach leader is inspired action that stands firmly on the side of positive, solution-oriented change.

Motivation #2—By becoming a coach leader, we are contributing to the transformation of our organization into a place where full-throttle engagement is more the norm rather than the exception. A place where robust business success can harmonize with each individual's need to find fulfillment and happiness at work. Coaching treats everyone as a human being, as an able adult, and as innovative and responsible colleagues.

Motivation #3—Applying the mental model and the skills of coaching in our relationship with ourselves and others permits us to become our best selves. We grow. We are transformed. And in so doing, we call forth in others their best selves as well. It's all about the relationships!

Motivation #4—Becoming a coach leader allows us to stop facilitating the craziness that can be found in many organizations today. Take back your power and change your experience; work within your circle of influence. Trade in same-old, same-old thinking for a new model of thinking, feeling, and behaving.

These possibilities take my breath away and I am committed to being a strong voice for such transformation. Join me and do all that you can from where you are. There is an absolutely inspiring quote from Margaret Mead, "Never doubt that a small, committed group of citizens can change the world. Indeed, it is the only thing that ever has!"[31] By continuing to work through the skills in this book and sustain them through intentionality as the "new you," you have become one of the "organizational citizens" who is changing the world. How good can we stand it?

Oh, and as a reminder, these next six coach leader behaviors are set up exactly like the four basic coach leader behaviors in the previous chapter: each one is set up in its own chapter-like space with an explanation of the behavior followed by examples that answer the question "now what," and end with Coaching TO GO suggestions.

Advanced Coach Leader Behavior #1:

Collaborative Inquiry

Because coach leadership is about helping others to access their own solutions to problems and challenges and generate their own options when faced with opportunities or dilemmas, we need to become really good at asking questions. And those questions need to come from our heart and a true desire to work together or *collaborate*. This is very different for most of us. We are used to quickly, definitively, and assertively advocating for our opinion—or "telling" the other person what to do (or not do).

Collaborative inquiry is a core skill that sets coach leadership apart from traditional management approaches. It is almost like being an organizational Sherlock Holmes. In the spirit of bringing out the best in others, we ask deliberate (carefully chosen) and meaningful questions that will get people thinking and moving forward on their own.

As a coach leader, we give people just enough to solve their own problems, create their own solutions, and then get out of their way. Asking questions is also really good for the person doing the inquiring. It is a reminder to practice humility and to avoid the assumption that we always know best or have the whole picture.

Remember, for the collaborative inquiry process to yield the kind of results that we all want, we must activate our coach leader ear through engaged, clear listening and be intentional in our choice of words, gestures, postures, sounds, tone, etc. We must all avoid the temptation to simply advocate for our own ideas, at least right away. There often is a point in time to offer our insights, experiences, and suggestions. But it is best to allow the other person(s) ample time to come up with their own solutions. We have an active role to play in that process. Coach leaders are not by-standers or hand-holders. We can make a vital contribution by asking relevant, high-quality questions—the more specific and intentional the question the better.

The initial step to mastering collaborative inquiry is to simply make it your habit to ask more questions. There are several different types of questions and all of them have a meaningful place in the collaborative inquiry process:

- Background Questions—These can introduce a topic, get the story behind a situation, and/or allow you to understand the context.

  Example: What is the medical history of this patient?

- Open-ended Questions—These invite others to explain, describe, explore, and/or elaborate.

  Example: Can you describe the problem with your computer?

- Close-ended Questions—These narrow the discussion to specific information.

  Example: What is the cost of this education program?

- Confirming Questions—These clarify understanding.

  Example: So, if your computer is upgraded this afternoon, you can complete the monthly census report by the end of the day on Friday?

- Coaching or Probing Questions—These go deeper into a situation or an issue. They have a coaching purpose. They are very intentional. They are the portal through which our colleagues can begin to develop their own solutions. We will discuss these in detail below as they are the backbone of collaborative inquiry and the coaching model itself. But I want you to consider this: because the questions of a coach leader are so specific and so intentional, they have spontaneity to them. They arise from what happens in a conversational moment with other people. Generic examples often don't do them justice.

That being said, I want to share with you what I consider to be one of the simplest, yet most powerful, questions that a coach leader can begin to use regularly. Ready? Here it is: "What do you think?" Followed by silence. Think about this elegant question. You are sending an important series of messages to the other person by using this question. It says, "You're smart and I value your opinion." It says, "I expect that you are thinking about this and have a solution to offer." It says, "You're a leader." Tom Peters provocatively states that these four words are the most important four words in business environments. And for me, it is no accident that they come in the form of a question.

Developing a habit of asking questions instead of giving into the temptation of telling, directing, avoiding, or even lobbying for our preferred solution is a *huge* first step. Concentrate on this discipline. It is important to acknowledge that, especially at first, it will take more time to ask questions and engage in collaborative inquiry. Being "charge neutral" or non-judgmental when asking questions is critically important. Consider these examples:

Charge Neutral Question: "What was your intention behind the email to Robert?"

Judgmental Question: "Why did you stir the pot and send Robert that provocative email?"

Charge Neutral Question: "What's the timeline that you typically follow for releasing meeting minutes?"

Judgmental Question: "Why are *you always* so late in getting out our meeting minutes?"

Sometimes, we convince ourselves that in the interest of time, we will take a short cut—just this once—and just tell someone what to do. And truly, there are legitimate circumstances when we *need to be* directive. But those times are exceptions. Remember, this is about "teaching a person to fish." Slow down to speed up.

Once you are in the rhythm of asking questions more often in everyday interactions to help others to gain access to their own answers, you are well positioned to begin to focus more intentionally on crafting really helpful coaching (probing) questions. At the same time, using the same foundation skills and core motivation (to help others to help themselves), you can begin to sprinkle **powerful coaching observations and requests** into your conversations as well.

In my experience, they are not used as frequently as coaching questions; nonetheless, they can be very useful under certain circumstances. And we want to be well-rounded in our coaching and have at our disposal a variety of skills and approaches. Being a coach leader isn't about following a script or reading down a checklist. It's about "dancing in the moment." It is not a one-size-fits-all leadership model—in fact, far from it. To be helpful and effective, we must remember that every one of our colleagues is unique and we must creatively discover the way to interact with them that best serves them as well as the organization (and you). We can't be "one trick ponies"! More on coaching observations and requests will follow. For now, let's continue our development and become masterful questioners!

Coaching questions share the following characteristics:

- They are slower rather than faster.

  Example: What did you do today to effectively lead from your seat?

- They go beyond simple inquiry. They are meaningful; they go deeper.

  Example: What evidence is there that Meredith is sabotaging your work?

- They make the other person stop and think for themselves.

  Example: What do you see going on in this project that's causing you to ask for a transfer?

  Example: If you were me, how would you approach this upcoming meeting?

- They are stated clearly and simply in a way that the other person can hear and understand using a charge neutral tone of voice.

  Example: How does gossip fit with our commitment to civility?

- They are often followed by silence to allow the question to really land with the other person and to allow them a few moments to think about their answer, their insight.

Example: From your perspective, what impact does your tardiness have on your teammates? (Silence.)

- They have a coaching purpose. There is a reason that you are asking this question at this time.

Example: How did storming out of the meeting help to resolve the conflict between you and Shirley?

Asking probing coaching questions may feel awkward at first if it is not your habit. Please stay with it! *This will encourage others to lead from their seat faster than almost anything else!*

Asking probing questions is the activation point for all of the foundation skills. Make this sticky through repetition. Work through those awkward moments—that's all that they are, awkward moments. With practice and determination, you will be the proud owner of a new valuable skill set. Valuable to the people around you, valuable to your organization and best of all perhaps—valuable to you. You will be positively changed.

Here is an example to illustrate the use of a coaching question in assisting someone to move forward:

"Mary" is a good colleague. She has chosen to work on improving a number of areas of her life and routinely shares information with you on her progress. One area on which she is working is becoming better organized and using time more effectively. As a part of that work, she is fostering new habits and challenging the way the she has done almost everything over the years. This is especially significant because, for much of her life, Mary has been a self-identified procrastinator.

One day in April, Mary approaches you and in an excited, animated way, shares with you that she has completed her research and has found a really terrific process to get more organized at work that seems right for her. She then goes on to tell you that her start date for engaging this new process is September 1. You are tuning in and listening clearly and taking it all in without interruption or judgment. You hear a sincere desire to change on Mary's part—to adopt a healthier, more productive way of managing her time and her space at the office. And yet, the start date that she has selected is pretty far in the future. Is this intentional and strategic? Is it procrastination? You may think that you know but you honestly don't.

If you were not working on becoming a coach leader, a success partner for people such as Mary, you might jump in and try to "fix" the situation with something like, "Why are you putting off your start date? You are such a procrastinator! You should start tomorrow if you are serious. I would if I were you!" However, a coach leader would approach this very differently. What two word coaching question would help Mary to stop and think about her decision in a clear but nonjudgmental way? My choice would be, "Why September?" Said in a charge neutral tone and followed by a brief silence.

For all you know, Mary has thought this through and knows that she has several months of nonstop travel that would interfere with her resolve to modify her current way of organizing her work life. Or, she could be falling into the familiar habit of putting things off. It is her work to determine that. By asking a powerful coaching question, you have given her the opportunity to stop and reflect and notice. She gets to decide what to do with this new insight! There is another situation analysis in the Coaching TO GO section of this chapter with which to practice. Give it a try!

Asking coaching questions also provides an ideal opportunity to accent the positive in workplace cultures and create engagement one conversation at a time. I want to share a questioning framework that does this very effectively. I have witnessed just how influential this understated approach can be. While there are many variations on it, the one that I have found most valuable and authentic was outlined by Kurt Wright in his book, *Breaking the Rules*.[32] This can be used to structure a staff meeting, a project update, your assessment of your own progress, or as an aid in helping someone else.

And again, while we are focused on the workplace, I can share that this particular skill yields amazing results with family, particularly teens and community groups. This is another example, for me, of big doors swinging on small hinges. I truly believe that if we were to use this approach more often in our everyday interactions, it would have a positive impact on our organization, our country, and the world. No, I do not consider myself naïve. This is a testament to how powerful I think that this can be!

Questioning Framework to Accent the Positive

There are many ways to approach coaching questions, but one of the most effective I have found is to ask questions in a way that accentuates the positive. I have found that the following list offers a framework to use to ask questions that stimulate positive action:

1. What are all of the things that are working?
2. How did all of these things end up working?
3. What's not right yet?
4. How can we make things even better?

Beginning any meeting or conversation with a firm focus on *what's working* creates a solid framework for building enthusiasm, confidence, and momentum for more. It gets us on a roll and moving in the right direction. Acknowledging successes is just one way of building and growing ourselves and those around us. And you may be surprised to discover just how many things are going right! Woo hoo!

The second question in the series is an interesting one. Why would we, as coach leaders, be keen on understanding how things got right? So that we can use that new insight to do those things more often in other areas or on other projects and, ultimately, get more things working. Sometimes, when we pause and think about how things got "right" we have a "V8 moment"—another way to say a blinding flash of the obvious based on an old commercial. Whatever you call them, they are so helpful in creating the strategies that bring success and satisfaction. It's a really good thing to catch our collective breath and notice them.

The third question is not simply a weasel word version of "what's wrong"! It is artfully structured to be heard and then interpreted very differently by our minds. Its gift is a sense that things can get right and that we are getting closer. This elegantly simple little question does more to connect us with our right brain innovative selves than most other tools and techniques. It releases us from fear and blame, and shifts our focus immediately to getting it right again.

Finally, the fourth powerful coaching question in the series calls on us to create a bigger vision. It relates to both those things that are working as well as those things that aren't working yet. It engages us in "futurethink." And it promotes belief in who and what we can become.

Now what? What can I do with my new understanding of this four-question framework that will make a difference at work and help me to lead from my seat?

How about shaking up one of your regular meetings in the same way that a colleague did at the Head Start program where he worked? Keith found the regular weekly staff meetings to be unproductive time-wasters. The team was in a rut, using the same agenda each week, and the meetings seemed to focus on all of the things that were wrong and who was to blame for each of them.

Initially, he dismissed the idea of using the four-question framework to generate a renewed sense of possibility because they weren't "his" meetings. When I asked him what that meant, he replied that he didn't lead the meetings or create the agenda! He was only an aide! I challenged that same-old, same-old thinking—it was an easy excuse for doing nothing. Instead, I asked him to lead from his seat at the meeting table, take a risk, and offer to prepare the agenda in advance and help to facilitate the discussion. He did (albeit skeptically) approach the director about doing something different. She was relieved to try something new that would engage the group differently.

The first time, the meeting went okay. The second and third times went even better and soon the energy of these meetings had shifted pretty dramatically. Later, the director acknowledged privately that she had not even recognized how destructive some of her comments had become over time. This is one for the win column!

Powerful Observations and Requests

As coach leaders, we know that one size does not fit all—not for people or situations. Meaningful observations and requests are complementary to asking questioning. There are times in the course of interactions when sharing something that we have observed is a more effective choice. Making an observation is done in the same charge-neutral way that we offer powerful questions. And they come from the same genuine spirit of wanting to help our colleagues to connect with and then reveal their very best selves at work. They also require us to be very intentional in our word selection. They can focus on some greatness that you are hearing or seeing.

Or observations can focus on something that, from your vantage point, is getting in the other person's way. They must be offered as your insight rather than the rule. You *must* tap into your intuition to get the timing right on these observations. It may sound cheesy, but timing is everything here.

Here is another simple illustration of a coach leader observation:

One of your colleagues, Ed, seems to be increasingly focused on what's wrong in the organization. Lately he has frequently portrayed himself and the team as victims or pawns of the corporate office, the downturn in the economy, and more demanding consumers. In a conversation today, Ed indicated that he/we were "like corks bobbing on the ocean at the mercy of 'them.'" Because you know and have a relationship with Ed, it might be right timed to say something such as: "It sounds to me as though you see yourself as pretty powerless right now." Then, simply practice silence for a minute or so. Let the next words belong to Ed. Your observation might surprise him—maybe he is not fully aware of his own message, either to himself or others.

Or perhaps he thinks that there is no other way to be. After all, doesn't everyone complain about their job?! This simple observation can be an opening for a conversation on what is within our control. It is my truth that we are all powerful and fully in charge of our own experience. Who knows what the actual impact of this simple, straightforward observation might be.

Coaching requests can be a valuable asset in coaching others. Powerful requests share the characteristics of coaching questions and observations. In addition, they typically focus on a bigger and bolder surge ahead. And right timing is also an essential here. Activate and then trust your intuition...your gut.

For example, Sam, you've talked about transferring to the European division to really challenge yourself for years. And yet it's never materialized. And here we are talking about it again. I'm going to be bold here and ask that you commit to making a plan to be in our Dutch office in one year from today.

Collaborative Inquiry is such a rich, powerful segment of our learning and is absolutely essential to the coach leader model and to **full-throttle engagement** that it deserves a summary. Here goes:

Coach leaders intentionally replace the habit of "telling people around us what to do" with the new habit of asking questions of others. This is immensely beneficial because it allows the other person to create their own solutions, to take moderate risks, to become more effective decision makers, and to more fully engage in the everyday life of the organization. Coaching questions are complemented by coaching observations and requests. They share the following characteristics:

- They always have a purpose beyond simply gathering information. They assist6 the other person and make a contribution to forward momentum.

- They often interrupt typical thought patterns—in other words, they can help people to free themselves from a "thought rut."

- They sometimes result in instant illumination—a "V8 moment" or a "blinding flash of the obvious."

- They genuinely have the potential to result in breakthroughs.

- They must flow from engaged, clear listening, especially tuning in fully to the other person, and intentional nonverbal messaging.

- They are always offered in a spirit of non-judgmentalism. They are not manipulative.

- They stem from connecting head, heart, and gut. They must be genuine and specific.

Coaching TO GO

1. **Another great book for your professional library**—Consider adding Kurt Wright's book, *Breaking the Rules,* to your collection of invaluable learning resources. I haven't found a better tool for practical application of What's Right questioning!

2. **Use what's right questioning**—Be intentional about using this simple collaborative inquiry tool in your everyday experience. It is effective in various venues: a crucial conversation, as the agenda at a staff or project status meeting, or in your own personal mastery work.

3. **Check out appreciative inquiry**—Leaders in the healthcare field, in particular, may want to learn more about appreciative inquiry. It is a philosophy for change that shares most features of collaborative inquiry. I have found it used most frequently in the nursing profession. My favorite source on this subject is a book written by Sue Annis Hammond, *The Thin Book of Appreciative Inquiry.*

4. **Become an intentional questioner**—Use intentionality to begin to ask more questions in conversations. Prepare for one-on-one and team meetings by jotting down a few coaching questions or observations for each situation. Ask the question. Practice silence. Then listen. Then repeat! Avoid the temptation to take the short cut of just telling someone what to do. Check in with yourself following the interaction and note what worked for you?

5. **Create your own "powerful questions" list**—Think about situations that you frequently encounter throughout your day. Then, create one or two coaching questions for each. Practice using them. Keep those that feel authentic and get the coaching results for which you are looking. Discard the rest. Add more questions to your personal repertoire. Share your list broadly within your workplace community. Consider having a central *bank* for coaching questions that everyone can access.

6. **Bonus Situation Analysis!**—Here is another example of col-

laborative inquiry in practice. I challenge you to create your own situation analysis to really make this skill stick in your life.

Situation: Karen is a nurse at the skilled nursing center that is part of the healthcare system. She is a "good" nurse and patients like her. She has a long standing habit of being late. She pledges to do things on time but never follows through. Others cover for her by doing her paperwork. But now they are becoming frustrated. She says that the patients come first and everything else has got to wait. You are the Administrator of the facility and you overhear several conversations on the subject this week. You have been personally working to help her to be more successful as a team member.

Identify one possible coaching question that may help Karen to move forward?

Identify one possible coaching request that may help Karen to move forward?

Identify one possible coaching observation that may help Karen to move forward?

Visit our website, www.vantage-inter.com for an example of each. Hint: You first! Create your own response before you review ours.

7. **Check out another short Tom Peters' video**—Visit YouTube or Tom's own website and watch the video titled, "4 Most Important Words."

Advanced Coach Leader Behavior #2:

Truth Telling and Truth Seeking

As we expand our application of the coach leader model, deepen our understanding of the skills, and grow more confident in our own ability to coach, we will find that we are becoming both truth tellers and truth seekers. What exactly does this mean and why is it important?

First, as coach leaders, we come to appreciate the fact that in interactions we often judge ourselves by our intention, while others judge us by their perception of what was said or done. So, to take an everyday work example, someone might tell us that something that we said in a meeting hurt their feelings. Many of us would quickly respond, "Well, I didn't mean (intend) to hurt you. I was being straightforward and making a point that I thought was important." There is an implication here that is often unspoken—since I didn't intend to hurt you, don't be hurt.

Sometimes we choose to become defensive. The other person may say, "Well, I AM hurt. And your words were the source!" Their perception is that because your words were hurtful to them that you must have meant them in that way or, alternately, that you should have known that it was a possible outcome. As coach leaders, we practice empathy more regularly as we consider the other person in our choice of words, body language, tone of voice, etc. We reduce the chance for misunderstanding by stating our intentions clearly and then checking in with the other person's perceptions.

Second, because our motivation is clearly to assist the other person, our colleague, and to help make the organization better in the process, we must be willing to take a moderate risk and tell our truth. Withholding our thoughts and feelings is counterproductive. And, similarly we are more prepared to hear others' truths about us and use them to improve ourselves.

Third, by building our leadership toolbox, we are now more capable of telling our truth in a way that the other person can hear it, let it in, and then do something constructive with it.

Fourth, the coach leader approach creates a safe space in which others can share their truth without fear.

Fifth, and perhaps most important, sorting out what is really "true" from interpretation, long standing organizational myths or sacred cows, and stale, old beliefs is vital to the change and growth process within healthy organizations. This is a hallmark of the coach leadership approach.

Sometimes, we have held on to a certain way of thinking or being for so very long that it feels as though it has to be that way. It feels like truth. I cannot count how many times I have visited organizations and been told that a certain process remains in place because "it has to...it is a regulation!" In almost every case, the process is the interpretation of a regulation, it is our response to a regulation, rather than the regulation itself. And interpretations can be changed!

Sixth and last, helping ourselves and others to sort truth from interpretation makes personal mastery easier. For most of us, it is easier to change something once we have acknowledged that it is only one (our) current interpretation. Once we recognize that something is not THE truth and not the truth for all time, we are a bit more willing to surrender it in favor of a potentially better way.

Now what? What can I do with my new understanding of truth telling and truth seeking that will make a difference at work and help me to lead from my seat?

Here's an example of how one person found the courage to tell himself and his boss "his" truth about a situation.

Garth works at an insurance company. A new team leader just joined the staff. She has a lot of new, good ideas. At the same time, she is turning off many people by using sarcasm in almost every conversation. She may simply be trying to be witty, but it's too over the top. Garth is secretly pleased a bit that she's stumbling. He had applied for the team leader position but was not the top candidate.

At this point, Garth has some choices. He can wait and see how things go. Maybe things will settle down and be okay. Or he could use intentional language to share his truth with the new team leader, in the sincere hope of helping her to fit in and do well in her new position. He could also be petty and join in the bashing of this new person. Finally, he could really stretch himself by telling himself the unvarnished truth about his feelings toward her. Perhaps he's jealous? Maybe hurt? Wanting to think the worst of her because he was not selected for the position?

Garth took the high road. He talked to the new team leader. He offered to help her. He also told her that he had been considered for her position too and was still down about not being selected. As they talked through these items, they started to develop a good working relationship that ended up benefiting them both—as well as the team's performance. Garth decided to use coaching behaviors to lead from his seat and engage in a caring, positive way.

Coaching TO GO

1. **Pay attention to conversations**—In the coming week, challenge yourself to be more intentional in your everyday conversations. Notice both intentions and perceptions. Begin to sort out truths. For example, when attending a meeting, notice how many "truths" there are on a given topic. Make some notes for yourself on what you learn.

2. **Use new language**—Begin to incorporate *intention, perception, my truth,* and *your truth* into your everyday conversations. This simple change can help you to maintain a new sense of awareness around truth telling. Using these words can also go a long way towards creating safety for another(s) and reducing defensiveness.

3. **Do a "safety" check**—How safe is it in your team/department/division or in the organization for team members to speak their truth? Conduct an informal survey and ask people for their sincere feedback on this incredibly meaningful item. What

might be getting in the way of more truth telling?

4. **Situation analysis**—Here is an opportunity for more skill building. It might be useful to use this as an exercise at a team meeting to stimulate meaningful conversation around truth telling.

    Bradley is the Director of a large in-house learning institute at a statewide non-profit association. He has recently spent a good deal of time building a new curriculum for staff. The initial plan was to conduct a three-day intensive program with the Vice Presidents and Directors and then provide individual assessments with each of their team leaders. The three-day program happened as planned. Two days later, Bradley's boss received a voice mail from the HR Director, a colleague of Bradley's, informing her that the team leaders did not want to engage in the individual assessment at this time. Bradley chooses to become immediately defensive and angry when given the news. He demands to know why they don't want to move forward. He also wants to call the HR Director and tell her how rude and unprofessional it was to call his boss instead of him with that type of message. You are Bradley's colleague and he has brought all of this to you so that you can assist him in taking a step back and re-evaluating the situation.

As a coach leader, what are your truths about all of this? From what you know, what seem to be some of Bradley's truths? As a coach leader, what would you choose to do to assist your colleague?

5. **Create Your Own Situation Analysis**—Let's get real. Create your very own situation analysis and use it as another learning exercise. The more relevant the learning, the stickier it will be.

Advanced Coach Leader Behavior #3:

Building Others

One of the most compelling reasons to use the coach leader model and one of its most valuable benefits is that the model calls on each of us to not only uncover the best in ourselves, but also to help those around us—including our boss, our colleagues, those who may report to us, and those that we encounter throughout our work day—to discover and embrace their best selves as well.

Once this virtuous cycle gets rolling in an organization, it feeds itself! I focus on your greatness and help you to see yourself through my eyes. You, in turn, are uplifted by the experience and mirror the experience back to me. This building behavior can become infectious and as it spreads, the cycle repeats itself. There comes a point when the energy of the organization changes to match the constructive energy of the building process. Then, the team as a whole is on a roll and becomes an amazing point of attraction for goodness and possibility. Now that's full-throttle engagement.

I have had the professional opportunity to be a part of such an organization. And I have watched it unfold in other organizations as a coach. It was magical. I want each of you to have that same experience.

In my coaching opinion, which has been shaped by hundreds of coaching observations and coaching conversations, one of the most interesting aspects of recognizing greatness in others and helping them to claim their best selves is that it is ***impossible to authentically recognize the greatness in another unless and until we acknowledge the greatness within ourselves.***

If you have not spent the time identifying, celebrating, and then cultivating your own greatness, you run the risk of missing the mark when highlighting the greatness in others. Your coaching comments may land on the other person as hollow or insincere. Remember, from our earlier conversations—you must begin working on yourself first. Coach yourself to greatness. Only then can you effectively help another(s). Revisit the chapters on the Coach Leader Model and Intentionality if you need to refresh and recommit.

I know that I am stating what is painfully obvious to most of us but it needs to be said—many of us show up to the workplace with defeating self-talk, lingering self-doubts, and a relatively limited view of who we are and what is possible. I am confident that as you have practiced intentionality more and more in your life and managed your thoughts, feelings, beliefs, and behaviors, that you have shed most of those same-old, same-old habits. But many of those around us each day have not yet started that work and are still stuck in a downward spiral. Remember, thoughts become things! It is true even if the thoughts are negative.

As you choose to build others around you, you will begin to notice that you more naturally see the brilliance in others. And want the best for them. I often hear, "I can't believe that I didn't see that in him before." Once you get the hang of this skill you will be amazed at how rewarding it is! It feels good and it is heartwarming to help someone else to turn on to and tap into their signature strengths! Often, we begin to see someone else's next level of achievement or their real potential before they do.

When we communicate clearly and authentically the vision that we have of others, we help them to capture that vision for themselves and believe more boldly in who they are and who they can become in the future. Building another simply means that we help others to, first, become aware of their positive attributes and then, use those attributes more and more frequently in thought, word and behavior in the workplace.

Building others is not one skill, but rather a constellation of mini (small but mighty) skills woven together to create powerful change. These mini skills are described below. They rely completely on action,.

clear listening and collaborative inquiry. The **Coaching TO GO** section contains exercises and suggestions for growing and sustaining these skills within yourself.

Mini Skills:

Assisting Others in Recognizing their Own Greatness—Many of my colleagues tell me that it is much easier to focus on the negative—or what is wrong with them—than appreciating their brilliances and uniqueness and celebrating their accomplishments at work and elsewhere. Our self-talk can be defeating and limiting. This often gets in the way of both our ability to craft a compelling vision for our future and our ability to move ahead and be our best selves. In other words, we can get caught in this downward spiraling conversation within ourselves. It's tough to break free from such a place.

As a coach leader, we have the privilege of helping others to claim the best that is in them. I affectionately call this "feed forward" (as opposed to feedback) because it can be so helpful in propelling us ahead!

Gradually, as we consistently hold up a mirror for the other person and as we choose to focus on their strengths, their own downward spiraling conversations will begin to recover and spiral up instead. Often, our colleagues feel a surge of energy as confidence increases and self- doubts decrease.

The way forward is a bit easier as old negative roadblocks are removed. Those around us may enjoy one or more of following benefits as a direct result of our willingness to consistently see the best in them and our help in allowing them to see it too:

- A new, more positive sense of self (a look in the mirror)
- New self-talk to match a new self-awareness
- More available energy
- More clarity and excitement about future opportunity
- Growing self confidence

To allow others to see themselves in a positive light as an individual with amazing potential, we must start with laying a sturdy foundation upon which they can build themselves. That means that through engaged, clear listening; intentional languaging; powerful questioning; and truth telling, we can

- Allow them to better understand who and where they are today and who and where they want to be in the future. This may mean that they consider what gives them satisfaction, how they define their own personal happiness, and what they identify as their source of passion. Being a coach leader is all about working in the critical gap—helping another to move from where they are today to where they want to be in the future.

- Remind someone that where they are today is "perfect enough," one part of their overall journey toward becoming her/his best self.

- Co-create with others possible ways to play to their brilliances and to leverage their strengths in the workplace.

When building another through coach leadership, we must be ever mindful of one of coaching's fundamental principles: it is a brilliance-based or strength-based leadership approach. We are called upon to spend the majority (80 percent) of our time, energy, and attention focused on *strengths,* our own and others.

The greatest good you can do for another is not just
To share your riches, but to reveal to him his own.

—Benjamin Disraeli

Building another also gives us the perfect opportunity to celebrate "the incomplete leader." In place of command and control, today's everyday leaders must be able to cultivate and coordinate the actions of others throughout the organization. They need to embrace the ways in which they are incomplete in order to be able to fill in their knowledge gaps with others' skills. Incomplete leaders differ from incompetent leaders in their ability to recognize their own growing edges (others refer to these as weaknesses) as well as strengths, and in having the confidence and humility to recognize unique talents and perspectives throughout the organization.

Deborah Ancona, in her article titled "In Praise of the Incomplete Leader," declares that "it's time to end the myth of the complete leader... Expecting leaders to do everything right, to be perfect, to be *complete*. No leader is perfect. The best ones don't try to be. They concentrate on honing their strengths and find others who can make up for their limitations."[33] This is what building others is all about. It creates leaders in every seat in the organization. Through it we create an interdependent web in the workplace that harmonizes strong business results with meaning and satisfaction.

Now what? What can I do with my new understanding of helping others to recognize their own brilliance that will make a difference at work and help me to lead from my seat?

Do what Carol did. She is the COO of a successful ambulance company in the southeastern U.S. She masterfully turned around the financial picture for the company in less than eighteen months. And she was a wiz at creating policies and procedures to tighten up operations. However, when it came to building key relationships with hospitals and nursing homes in their service area, she was out of her comfort zone.

It was hard to accept that she wasn't all that good at connecting with people. She intentionally chose to see this as an opportunity to allow another person in the organization to really shine and grow. She arranged a lunch with Devon, the Director of Marketing. She had come to admire the ease with which he developed relationships and his good stewardship of them once they were in place. She asked him to be her partner in forging new alliances in the market place. He eagerly agreed and he took the lead with a passion. She learned a great deal from working with Devon. She developed relationships too. But she continued to recognize Devon's contribution and encouraged him to do more. Devon independently developed an in-house course on building great relationships, which he proudly delivered himself many times.

Several years later, Devon left the company to take on a more senior position with an international marketing firm. Building this young leader, making room for his seat at the leadership table, and practicing humility helped everyone involved. This is also an example of the power of followership.

What's right questioning? In the previous coach-leader behavior on collaborative inquiry, I talked about a framework for asking questions that accentuates the positive. The "what's right" questioning framework can also be a useful ally when it comes to assisting others in unleashing their best selves at work. Think about it. What better way to initiate or expand a conversation on someone's greatness than by reviewing all of the things that are working or going well in that person's experience? Conversely, when something is not going well, one of the most powerful ways to turn the situation around is to ask "what's right" as opposed to finding fault and making everyone and everything wrong.

Because "what's right" questions are so instrumental in successful coach leadership, I am repeating them here to refresh your memory:

What are all of the things that are working?

How did this happen?

What's not right yet?

How can we make things even better?

At times our own light goes out and
Is rekindled by a spark from another person.
Each of us has cause to think with deep gratitude
Of those who have lighted the flame within us.
—Albert Schweitzer

Affirming and Communicating Belief—As you may have noticed by now, the mini skills of building another person are very, very simple. In fact, they are deceptively simple. They might seem too small or even insignificant to make a difference in our relationships with others. And we might dismiss them out of turn. That would be unfortunate.

While these mini skills are simple, they can have a major impact on someone else. This is the case with affirming and then sharing your belief in someone else. Knowing that you believe that someone is special in their work life and that you have confidence in their abilities and in who they are can give that person the turbo charge that they need to surge forward. Or it just might provide that one extra ounce of confidence that they need to reach a milestone or overcome an obstacle that has haunted them for some time.

Right about now, some of you may be thinking "my colleagues know that I believe in them…I don't need to say it out loud." Others have told me that it sounds corny or condescending to tell someone that you believe in them. "I can't say that to my boss or to my peer!" As a coach who has spent a great deal of time *listening* in many different types of organizations, I can tell you that these are not my truths. People around us need to hear regularly that we believe in them. It never gets old if offered sincerely. They stand just a bit straighter. They do just a bit more. They take a larger risk. They play bigger.

This example demonstrates just how simple this behavior can be in interactions. *Your colleague at work has just been promoted to a very visible, very prestigious position. Initially, she was filled with confidence. After two months of challenges, however, she is increasingly filled with doubts and fear that she cannot be effective in the job. You are 100 percent certain that she can do the job and more. The simple gift of telling her that—specifically and emphatically—could be the turning point for her to gain traction and move forward.*

Sorting the past/present/future—The final mini skill to building someone is to assist them in properly sorting the past from the present and the future. Many times, the best of us can get stuck thinking that the past necessarily predicts the future. It doesn't, by the way. We can change. We can choose a different behavior. We can grow a different habit.

As a coach leader in our organization we can help others by reminding them that *our point of power is in the present moment.* We cannot change the past but we can definitely learn from what happened. One of my favorite quotes from Mother Theresa was a response that she gave when criticized for changing her position on some issue. She simply said, "I didn't know then what I know now." How simple. How elegant.

Similarly, through intentionality, we become architects of our own future. How we choose to think, feel, and act in the present will, in large measure, shape our future. That means that we are in the driver's seat when it comes to our own experience. Helping others to see this and to act from this knowledge will allow them to reclaim their own personal power and make strides to being at their best at work.

Now what? What can I do with my new understanding of sorting past/present/future that will make a difference at work and help me to lead from my seat?

Here's how you can put this behavior into action immediately to help your organization reach full- throttle engagement: Your teammate at work went through a particularly difficult period of time about a year ago. She behaved poorly at work, made some bad decisions, and was on probation for a short period of time as a result. She hasn't had any similar incidents in over a year and has done some great work since then. She wanted to apply for another position internally but has decided against it because she is sure that everyone sees her as a screw up. You can help her to sort out the past from the present and the future. That doesn't mean that you excuse her past behavior. Rather, ask what she has learned from it. Remind her that she can only act in the present. Encourage her to talk frankly with the person posting the open position and to tell her truth about her behavior. Use coaching questions to assess her willingness to create a future that is different from the past. It may only be a ten minute conversation but it could help her to change course. Everyday leadership in action.

Coaching TO GO

1. **Focus on strengths/brilliances**—Do you truly have a handle on what your own signature strengths are? How about your team members' strengths? What proportion of your time, energy, and attention is focused on amplifying your own and others' brilliances? Deepening our appreciation and understanding of the greatness around us will help us to build ourselves as well as our colleagues. This is not a one-size-fits-all assignment. We must see one another through different lens. A best practice from one high performing team that I know is to identify the

brilliances of oneself as well as each member of the team *and share* those observations and experiences *openly.* Here's a challenge: Pick one person per day and simply list the assets and positive, helpful qualities that s/he has.

2. **Check out strengths finder**—Visit the website, www.strengthsfinder.com to evaluate the tools and techniques offered through this best-selling leadership system.

3. **Deploy "what's right questioning"**—Identify an opportunity this week, to experiment with this simple, yet powerful, five question framework. Evaluate its contribution to building others.

4. **Read the article**—Visit our website, www.vantage-inter.com, to find a copy of Deborah Ancona's provocative article, "In Celebration of the Incomplete Leader." Read the entire article with your team and have a group discussion about letting go of being perfect in favor of playing to one another's strengths.

5. **Mini skills practice**—Take each of the mini skills that make up **building others** and make it your own by actively using each one and informally evaluating the results.

6. **Situation analysis**—Here is a chance to put your learning to the test. What building skills would you use (if you were Norm) in this situation and why?

    Dolores is a long term member of your team. She has been promoted over the years and is now in a more senior position. Norm is the COO. He likes Dolores and thinks that she does a decent job. She is very loyal. Reliable. Pleasant. But he has thought for a while that she is holding back—she could really be so much more in the organization. Every time he thinks that she is breaking through to a new level, it doesn't materialize. He mentioned something to her once, but she seemed embarrassed by the attention. With his renewed commitment to being a coach leader, particularly building others, he wants to come at this opportunity with new energy. What would you do if you were Norm?

7. **Create your own situation analysis**—Develop a situation analysis from the real experiences of your organization.

Advanced Coach Leader Behavior #4:

Growing Others

At the boundaries, life blossoms.
—James Gleick, *Chaos*

Growing others is a coaching principle that flows naturally as a complementary next step to building others. It derives its power, in part, from the momentum created by the building process. It can be one of the most gratifying experiences that coach leaders have. Having been on hundreds of professional journeys with my executive coaching clients, I can testify to the fact that it is a personal pleasure and a professional privilege to play my part in someone else's success strategy.

Helping another person to stretch and grow means that, through our collaborative relationship with them, they find the courage to leave their comfort zone and dare to reach for the next level of their own potential. A dear friend of mine, who has a quirky saying for every occasion, has told me repeatedly, "If you're not stretching and growing, you're dead!"

Her point is that we humans never get the work of learning and developing done. I call it being "joyfully unfulfilled." For me that means that we can be genuinely satisfied and grateful for who we are and where we are in the moment and also eagerly want more.

As coach leaders, it is our responsibility to care enough about those around us to engage with them in the growth process. If we want to have workplace community and bring out the boss in everyone, then we have got to want people around us to reach their potential as much as we want that for ourselves.

Coaching others on personal and professional growth requires that we fire on all cylinders and use all of the foundational coaching skills—clear listening, intentional languaging, and purposeful, powerful questioning. We need to check in with ourselves regularly to be certain that our motives are pure. We genuinely want to help someone else to be their best because it is really a great accomplishment for them and gives them an advantage in their lives rather than us being manipulative, for example, to subtly get someone to do what we want them to do.

What greater wealth is there than
To own your life
And to spend it on growing?
—Ayn Rand

Professional growth (and personal growth for that matter) typically involves the following core elements. We need to be fully aware of these as we work on growing ourselves as well as helping others to do the same.

- **Risk**—Growth is not about playing it safe. It requires that we dare to move beyond the boundaries and limitations that hold us in our current habits and performance levels. It can be scary and exciting at the same time. I have often reiterated a Tom Peters' line to my coaching clients, "I would rather have a bold failure than a mediocre success." [34] So many professionals that I have met are afraid to venture beyond their comfort zones because they believe that there will be negative consequences, real or perceived, if they fail. They settle for very modest progress instead. With some exceptions, playing small does not generally serve us or our organizations.

- **Expansion**—In some way or another, professional growth involves expansion. We move to the next level of performance in an area. We do more of something. We become more effective at something, perhaps requiring less time or resources. Or we breakthrough and come up with a completely new and better way of being or doing. Maybe we begin to think at a more strategic level. Although it may seem counterintuitive, expansion can also be experienced by doing LESS of something. For example, if it has been our habit to micromanage our team, then fostering trust and accountability by intentionally staying out of the "detailed hows" could be evidence of significant growth and expansion, even though we are pulling back and doing something less often.

- **Visioning**—As I pointed out in chapter 4, Stephen Covey tells us that one of the habits of highly effective people is to *begin with the end in mind*.[35] This is particularly true for situations involving professional growth. We must have a clear and specific destination in our minds. We must stand ready to help others craft their own destination and determine their own route to get there. What is the desired future? What will it look like? How will the person feel when it is accomplished? How badly does the person want the outcome? Creating a vision and then holding it vividly in one's mind is essential to professional growth.

- **Making change stick**—Let's face it, an individual's growth is about internal change (changing our thoughts, feelings, beliefs), and external change (changing behavior, interactions). Part of the growth process is to keep our new habits alive so that they become a permanent part of our experience.

- **Intentionality**—Woven into each of the other core elements of the professional growth cycle is a heightened awareness and then increased choicefulness. In other words, intentionality! Intentionality is the energy conductor that allows growth to happen. It's what gives us the courage to create and then hold onto a bigger picture of ourselves. It allows us to take that leap of faith and risk going where we haven't gone before. And it is the Velcro that makes change stick.

As coach leaders in our organizations, we must make a commitment to helping those around us to intentionally grow. Again, before we can effectively help someone else to identify their path forward, we must engage in that work ourselves. When it comes to professional growth, the "do what I say not what I do" approach will be unsuccessful. It is my truth as your coach that you and I cannot challenge our colleagues to grow and learn unless we are modeling that behavior ourselves. A huge credibility gap will be painfully apparent to everyone. The moral here is, you first. Demonstrate the power of growth by growing yourself.

As you might guess, leading others and truly challenging them on professional growth is at the very heart of coach leadership and full-throttle engagement. These coaching conversations contain more challenges and are riskier. You could miss the mark and there are consequences when that happens. But the rewards when you hit the mark are worth the risk. It's all about not settling for good, not getting too comfortable where you are, and busting through barriers and obstacles into a steady stream of forward progress through action. Whereas building others needs a gentler, more subtle, supportive, and encouraging leadership approach, helping others to stretch and grow themselves depends on an edgier, focused coaching presence. It may be even trickier when the other person is our boss or our peer. We must challenge others, yet in a way that will land constructively with them. We must really tap into our intuition to know when to press and when to pause. But you've come this far, so keep forging ahead and becoming more masterful. Never abandon the coach leader starter skills. Risk making an honest mistake. Keep learning.

Just as the "building others" coach leader behavior is actually made up of several mini skills so too is "growing others." Combining these with truth telling and truth seeking is essential to success. These mini skills are identified and individually discussed below:

Mini Skills

Intent and Commitment—As coach leaders, we must be committed to be of service to our colleagues as they develop and then follow their plan for professional growth. One way to do that is to regularly check in with our colleagues on their intentions as well as their continued commitment to transforming themselves and moving ever closer to their best selves. While the work always remains theirs to do, we can help them to hold their picture of their future clearly in their minds and remain focused on the benefits that they will receive when that vision becomes their next reality. Helping someone to remember, re-choice and re-commit is particularly helpful to use when someone

- is going through a difficult period of time
- is working through obstacles that may have been in their way for a very long time or
- is simply worn down or fatigued.

Revisiting the intention that they created when they began their work and making an ongoing commitment to doing what it takes to get there could be that final booster rocket that they need to break through to a new level of performance. It can reignite their passion for the outcome; it can allow them to see the journey—the good times as well as the challenges—through a different lens; it can provide the courage to persevere. And knowing that they are not completely alone in this work, that you and others in the organization are their success partners, can make the difference.

Revisiting someone's intent and commitment can also serve as an opportunity for them to make a mid-course correction if that is what is in their best interest. Perhaps circumstances have changed and they are no longer excited by their vision or their goals. It is also possible that as someone learns more about their desired outcome—for example, a university degree in a particular field—there may be new insights that lead the person in a new direction.

As coach leaders, our role is not to judge which path is right or wrong for our colleague; that remains their decision. It is our responsibility to help them to be truthful with themselves, to continue to grow as a person by learning lessons from their experiences, and to be fully present in the moment and make intentional decisions. Remember, assisting others with their professional growth often means that we challenge our colleagues, hold them accountable to their word, and tell our truth about what we see and sense. Growing others requires us to get out on the limb at times. But the risk is worth it because our colleagues are worth it.

Consider this example:

Imagine that you know someone who has worked their way up through the ranks, from dishwasher to supervisor of the kitchen staff at a large hotel/restaurant. Dale has set her sights on becoming the head chef and has earned a position in a very competitive culinary program. This course of study is very demanding. With her current job responsibilities and going to school at night, Dale is really running out of gas. She is weary and wants to quit with only six months left in her program. By using a coaching question or two and practicing silence, you can quickly help her to clarify her ongoing commitment to landing that head chef's position. You might say, "What made you so determined to become the head chef in the first place?" Then you use silence and allow her to tell her story. You can observe that two of her signature strengths are perseverance and resilience. Make a request and ask her to tell you of a time when her perseverance paid off. Perhaps you can ask her what her current level of commitment is to the chef position. Listen! Never be judgmental or opinionated. You are simply helping your friend to help herself. She can make her own decisions. You are allowing her to see the whole picture, rather than the brief snapshot of this moment and how she feels. It may well be temporary.

Encourage "Bigness"

There are times when helping others to grow means that we must shake things up a bit. During the growth process, there may be times when a person plateaus.

Anyone who has ever been on a weight-loss program or a fitness regime knows what I mean. The person makes substantial progress and then levels off with little or no progress. Sometimes, a person may begin to coast or become too comfortable and lose the momentum with which they started. In other circumstances, someone may begin to experience fear as they play at higher and higher performance levels.

These are all typical reactions and, occasionally, they can be useful. For example, if we are coasting along for a short period of time in order to recharge our batteries or clarify our direction, then that is an intentional course of action and creates value. It ultimately could help us to move forward quicker—slowing down to speed up! If, on the other hand, we are doing it unconsciously or because we are scared, then it is most likely not contributing positively to our progress. There are also times when someone is simply "in the flow" and can take on bigger challenges with ease. All they need is a nudge in that direction.

As coach leaders, we must remember to tap into our intuition at these intersections. If we sense that someone can actually dial it up a notch, then we must hold up a mirror for our colleague to allow them to see what we see and issue a professional dare! We must always remember that this person is his/her own expert and will make the final decision. As their success partner, we can encourage them to play bigger and bolder. For example, if one of our colleagues had set a goal to make five new sales per month and she is meeting that goal quickly and easily for three months, then we might offer the following: "Wow, I noticed that you have met your goal each month this quarter. Congratulations! And it looks as though it has been pretty easy for you. Is that so? Why not make your goal bigger? Would you be willing to change your goal to making seven new sales per month?"

When encouraging expansion, I often ask my coaching clients to "shoot for the stars and settle for the moon." Rarely will someone who chooses to take me up on my challenge miss their new goal!

Speed Things Up

Similar to "encouraging bigness," there are times in our relationship with others around us when we have the opportunity to challenge their same-old, same-old thinking about time. Coach leaders must offer healthy challenges to those around us when it comes to helping someone else to change and grow.

If we become aligned with our own inner coach, our intuitive self, then we will more and more frequently sense when to encourage someone else to turn up that burner and achieve that goal faster than they had originally thought was possible. This can be an incredible moment in someone's journey—a breakthrough when they more fully appreciate their highest self and what is possible for them.

In these situations, we must always be aware of the boundaries of our role as a coach leader and remember the essence of the coaching framework. Daring someone to move toward their goal faster is not about telling them or forcing them to do it at that pace. The decision and the energy must be theirs to allow the work to be as sustainable as possible. They must own it fully. Asking someone to shorten the timeline for achieving something may sound something like:

I know that you originally thought that getting your Master's degree would take a full three years. The enthusiasm and the passion that you're displaying as part the experience makes me think that you can get there in half the time! You are really on fire. Is it time to rethink that original timeline? Imagine how you would feel if you were walking down the aisle wearing your cap, gown, and that huge smile of yours in December?

When it comes to creating a timeline, we have legitimately learned to pad the schedule. In other words, we add some time to allow for unanticipated situations. Asking someone to quicken their pace for achieving their goal may feel like asking them to work without a safety net. That's not necessarily a bad thing; we must simply be aware of what feelings might surface for the other person.

A word of caution here: the other person remains in the best position to consider the dare and either take it, modify it, or pass on it. And as a coach leader, we are not entitled to feel disappointed or even slighted if our colleague chooses another course of action. You have made a contribution simply by putting it out there. Now we are called upon to surrender it and continue to support the other person unconditionally.

Slow Down to Speed Up

Counterbalancing requests to *quicken the pace* are requests to slow things down. Both can be powerful forces in the growth cycle and both have earned a legitimate place in your coaching tool box. Blindly adhering to a schedule is not helpful. If there is new information or new circumstances to consider, then it is important to pause to collect one's thoughts and then go on intentionally. In other cases, investing the time to strategize, re-consider, and/or celebrate milestones along the way can return huge dividends and get you across that final finish line quicker and easier. It may sound oxymoronic but it is my truth as a coach. Of course, this is not the same as procrastination, coasting, or avoiding. If we sense that these are the forces behind our colleague's decision, this requires a different kind of coaching conversation. Tame your own impatient self and encourage others to do the same. Then, reap the benefits!

Ask for an Extreme

Yes, there are extreme sports, extreme games, and, even, extreme coaching requests—at least when it comes to helping others to change and grow. Don't be fooled by the name of this mini skill! Challenging someone to go for the extreme does not necessarily mean that you are asking them to do more. For sure, there are times when we just sense that someone we care about can really stretch into something amazing and we do encourage them to be or do something really big and hairy and audacious.

There are also many times when we ask for extreme behavior from someone that involves doing something or being something less. For example, one of my wonderful organizational clients regularly operates at a pace darn close to frantic. Asking for the extreme from them often means that I encourage them to take a pause between projects to debrief, gather learning moments, and celebrate success. At first, this was a difficult request for them to honor. After all, there was so much more to do and so little time! Now, they have gained an understanding, through their own experience, of the value of catching their collective breath. Can you think of a situation that you face today in which asking for the extreme from someone (or even from yourself) would involve actually doing something less? Think about it.

Robin is an intern in your department. You have been asked to assume the formal role of her individual coach during her year with the company. She is so enthusiastic. She can dominate a conversation at a meeting. The good news is that she is confident in her abilities. The bad news is that she doesn't know when to be quiet. She interrupts, talks over people, and feels as though she is demonstrating positive business assertiveness. In your weekly check in meeting, you tell her your truth about this behavior—that it is doing more to hurt her than help her—and challenge her by asking her for the extreme: not to volunteer a single comment during the next staff meeting. To listen clearly and take notes. To appreciate others' approaches. And to then share what she learned from the experience with you. Appreciating the balance between listening and speaking is one of area of growth for many of us. It also reminds us that followership is an important part of leadership. This would be a powerful coaching request—asking for the extreme. In this case, the extreme part refers to not doing something.

Offer a Framework for Personal Accountability (Understanding & Accepting Consequences)

When it comes to growing others, this final mini skill is "first among equals." Growing is a demanding process that requires substantial time, energy, and attention. Assisting someone in this area means that you, as a coach leader, must match that level of intensity and energy. Remember, coaching is **not** an "I'm okay, you're okay, anything goes" approach to individual or team performance. One of the finest gifts of the coaching space that is created in an organization when the coach leader model is universally practiced is that it offers a framework for personal accountability. Yes, coaching gives us the opportunity to "do the right thing in task and interaction." It is our responsibility as a coach leader to combine this framework of accountability with intentional languaging and truth telling so that there is a *crisp, shared understanding and acceptance of the consequences* for our actions or inactions.

This applies equally to situations in which we are interacting with our boss, our peers, our team members, or even ourselves. All organizations and all relationships have rules, regulations, procedures, processes, and boundaries. We must make ourselves smart about what these are and honor them. In the most tightly regulated, buttoned down organization, there is still plenty of room for growth, inspiration, and innovation. When it comes to holding a framework of accountability, one of the most important jobs that we have as a coach leader is to call others out on, what I call, "snap backs." When we observe someone engaged in either old, maladaptive behavior or thinking or not following through on a commitment, it is our responsibility to identify this pattern or habit for them—hold up our mirror and let them see the situation through our eyes.

It is equally important for you to send a clear, consistent message that encourages others to do the same thing for you. In some circles,

this snap back to old ways of thinking is referred to as "stinkin' thinkin."
This means that we are back in a pattern of thinking or acting that is
working against us and the organization as a whole, rather than for us!

Coaching TO GO

1. **Combine skills for maximum impact**—Develop one coaching question for each of the basic growing skills noted above.

2. **Practice self-coaching**—Intentionally use the basic growing
skill set to achieve one of your own professional goals. You first!

3. **Be bold**—Building someone requires that we assert ourselves
more as coach leaders. This coaching skill requires more power
and more maturity as a coach. So, if you have been working
through the material diligently, now is the time to take a risk. Be
challenging. Use all of the skills that you acquired in the starter
kit as well as the basic coaching skills that you have most recently
added to your repertoire. Listen intently to your own intuition.
Coach leadership is about challenge. It's all about growth. Don't
be a bystander while others around you play it safe. Here's
your coaching challenge: carefully reflect on each of the skills
involved in *Growing Others*. Next, identify one current situation
that you believe would benefit from the application of each of
them (one unique situation for each of the skills). Pre-pave or
plan how you will apply each of the skills to the situation. Bring
all of the other coaching skills to the experience. Remember
your engaged, clear listening, intentional languaging, collaborative inquiry, truth telling, and building skills. Now, go forth and
play big as a coach leader in your organization. This has never
been about being perfect. If you are waiting to use your newly
acquired skills until you have them down perfectly, it will be a
long, long wait! We are shooting for "perfect enough." As you
take risks as a coach leader, learn from each experience. That
is part of your own growth!

4. **The acceleration trap**—Learn more about *Slowing Down to
Speed Up* by reading another Harvard Business Review article
titled, "The Acceleration Trap." This great article was written by

Heike Bruch and Jochen Menges and has provided meaningful learning for a number of my clients.

5. **Take advantage of the AdVantage Coaching System**—Our very own AdVantage Coaching System is a powerful way for growing oneself and others. Consider using it for your own professional development as well as gifting it to other team members and colleagues. It is discussed in more detail in Chapter Eight, Coaching Pathways. Also, visit the Vantage website, www. vantage-inter.com, for more information and to place an order.

6. **Ask for feedback**—Now is the perfect time to check in with team members, your boss, and other colleagues to get some feedback on your application of coach leader skills. This is yet another opportunity for you to GROW as well. Push through fear and limiting beliefs about who you are in your organization!

7. **Call out snap backs**—Are you tolerating unhealthy behavior in yourself? In others? Answer this powerful coaching question authentically. Be a truth teller. If the answer is yes, develop a plan to address it courageously.

8. **Situation analysis**—Work through this situation analysis to sharpen your ability to help others stretch and grow!

    You are a leader of a group in a financial organization. The amount of work required of your team has increased steadily over the past few years and shows no sign of slowing down. While this work is exciting and very positive, there are some behaviors that are becoming problematic as the company grows in size and sophistication. It is difficult for you to pinpoint the cause. However, the outcome is that people miss deadlines, don't seem to "get on board" with new practices, and sometimes you have to ask several times for information and reports. Overall, this group is doing amazing work but these problems are holding the organization back. How do you assist your team to grow to the next level of performance?

9. **Create your own**—It's your turn to put together one or more situation analyses based on real life experiences at work. Take

the time to do this work—it can fast forward your mastery of this skill set tremendously. Make the learning relevant by applying it directly to situations that you face today! Use the space at the end of the chapter to make it happen.

Advanced Coach Leader Behavior #5:

Setting and Achieving Goals

> *The best time to plant a tree is twenty years ago.*
> *The second best time is now.*
> **—Ancient Chinese Proverb**

Coach leadership is not a contemporary business version of the "I'm okay, you're okay" self- help approach that was in vogue for a period of time in the late 1960s and 1970s. It is an action- oriented tool for assisting us all to move from where we are today to where we want to be in the future. In order to close this critical gap, we identify inspired actions and navigate our way through them. In other words, coach leadership is an ideal vehicle and creates an optimal space to help ourselves and others to set and achieve personal and/or professional goals.

When it comes to setting and achieving goals, the role of the coach leader (and, remember, we are all coach leaders) is to help those around us to develop a plan to identify and meet one or more goals. A coach leader provides wholehearted support and encouragement—a safe structure in which to work the plan and a committed partner to ask the tough questions that could make the difference between average and extraordinary. This is where the rubber hits the road in coaching. Coaching is results-oriented. It is about major change. Assisting others to successfully reach and then exceed their goals requires that we use all of the coach leadership tools and techniques that we have assembled in our toolbox.

Think about goals that you have had or changes that you have wanted to make in yourself. Were there times when it was difficult to even determine the first step to take? Or maybe you ran out of steam half-way into a plan for change and could not get yourself "unstuck." How about occasions when your plan wasn't working and you couldn't see how to turn things around?

We've all been there. The difference is that we have something up our sleeves that we didn't have before: a powerful set of skills that we can use to help ourselves and our colleagues to create the sparks of possibility to get started and the energy to navigate around or through obstacles and create breakthroughs. Say it with me: we are coach leaders, the superheroes of organizational cultures. Maybe we should call ourselves "culture heroes!"

Some self-confronting questions:
Where do I want to be at any given time? How am I going to get there?
What do I have to do to get myself from where I am to where I want to
be? What's the first step I have to take to get moving?
—George A. Ford

Together, let's examine how coaching can be a positive influence at key intersections along the journey to setting and achieving our goals.

Goals—A Personalized Blueprint

One of the ways that we can help others to move forward rapidly in their lives is to hold them accountable for planning and documenting their vision, goals, inspired actions, schedule, and identifying their rewards. This document goes by several names: a personalized blueprint, a roadmap to your chosen destination, or an individual master plan.

There are many solid resources, including software, that coach you on how best to create or arrange this tool so that it is easy to use and does its job of helping you to track your progress. In my coaching approach, the AdVantage Coaching System, we call it the Tune-In Tune-Up Blueprint. The point is for you to encourage your colleagues to find a tool that feels right to them and that they are willing to use regularly. Or create one to their own liking.

Each person's journey is a very unique experience. Each of us gets to "have it our way" when it comes to keeping us on track. One of the most innovative approaches that I have come across so far, came from the creative process of one of my MBA classes. As their course project, one team created a career version of "Chutes and Ladders" called "Chutes and Leaders" (don't you agree that it is an innovative idea?). You moved along your very own "talent plan" with inspired actions that allowed you to move far ahead and attempted to avoid missteps that sent you back. This example demonstrates how to blend advanced coach leader skills for maximum results. This one helps us to set and achieve goals through playfulness, another behavior covered in detail in this chapter beginning on page two hundred. Gaming allows your right brain—your imagination center—to help you with the mostly left brain planning process.

In addition to the AdVantage Coaching System, my favorite tracking tool comes from Jack Canfield's book, *The Power of Focus*. You might want to check it out.

Develop a plan

One of my coaching biases is that memorializing something in writing (or electronically on your technology) makes it real and begins to activate the thoughts and feelings that you will need to make progress. For me, it is an imperative for those of us who have both intention and resolve when it comes to our goals to create a comprehensive plan to make it happen. A basic plan includes the following key elements:

- A clear, crisp statement of exactly what the goal(s) is.
- An exhaustive list of the inspired actions that are needed to achieve the goal.
- A specific schedule to accomplish these actions.
- An equally exhaustive list of the resources that will be needed to achieve the goal.
- A structure to create and sustain the energy to take step after step over time.
- A way to measure progress and achievement—how will we know when our work is complete?

- A reward system—How will we intentionally celebrate along the way? How will we reward ourselves for sticking to the plan?

There are many great resources to structure a plan: templates, master plans, books, blueprints, etc. I will share my favorites in the Coaching TO GO section for this behavior. Simply know that you don't have to reinvent the wheel here. If it feels good to tailor make a structure just for you, then do it! If not, use something that has worked for others.

Coach leaders have an active role to play in this planning process, although it is important to remind ourselves that this is not our work; therefore, we do not own someone else's plan. They do. Using powerful coaching questions and observations and building skills, we can help others to:

- Develop the elements mentioned above
- Evaluate the plan to be certain that it can act as a roadmap to get us where we want to be
- Identify challenges and strategies for dealing with them
- Make a solid, lasting commitment to the work

Work the Plan

Being a coach leader is no less vital in the implementation phase, when someone begins to take the inspired actions that the plan calls for. Here, active, engaged listening; powerful questioning and observing; and growing the other are often the coaching tools that we will reach for to be most helpful. Don't overlook the role that play can have in making someone's goal come to life. While work is most definitely involved, creativity, day dreaming, and innovative thinking can lighten the load of a plan and catapult someone forward. Play as a coaching tool is discussed next, so do consider its place in goal achievement by reading ahead.

Rarely is working toward a goal a straight shot. By that I mean a steady, forward trajectory from where you were to where you want to be. Instead, it usually feels more like two steps forward and one step back. Progress can surge forward at times or we can experience snap backs that can send us back to the starting line. Limiting thoughts can creep in if we are not intentional. Our feelings can take on the characteristics of a roller coaster ride—hopeful and energetic one minute and frustrated and dejected the next.

Can you sense how powerful it can be to have a colleague by your side to gift you with the generosity of spirit, the belief and affirmation, the truth telling, and the accountability and inspiration of the coach leader? It is my firm belief that if we did more of this for each other (and ourselves) we would create better workplace communities, which in turn, would lead to all kinds of good stuff!

Helping someone on this journey to achievement focuses primarily in the following areas:

- Reminding him/her that none of us are alone in this journey and that others want him/her to succeed and are rooting from the sidelines. Reaffirming that we are in this together and that the partnership is a strong one.
- Re-choicing regularly by recommitting to the goal and keeping it foremost in her/his mind.
- Evaluating progress/momentum and inventing mid-course corrections if necessary.
- Innovating when something seems to get in the way.
- Practicing fearlessness regularly.
- Keeping the focus.
- Accelerating or decelerating when circumstances change.
- Recognizing and calling out procrastination and other old habits.
- Celebrating along the way!

Helping others to achieve has to be one of the most satisfying rewards of fostering the coach leader in us all. It is legacy work—a fit that continues to give for a very long time. Try it, you'll like it! The Coaching TO GO section below will help you to get started.

Now what? What can I do with my new understanding of setting and achieving goals that will make a difference at work and help me to lead from my seat?

This coaching behavior is one that must be first applied to the relationship that you have with yourself before assisting others around you.

You coach you first! Do you have a talent plan, a blueprint for becoming your best self at work? For activating the principles of coach leadership day in and day out? For leading from your seat regularly and doing more than the minimum expected? If the answer is no or not yet, then now is the moment to get that work done. Remember, the present moment is the point of power.

Next, encourage others to do the same. For example, you may identify with the sales representative who had a colleague who always expressed "hope" that she would get a transfer to the New York City store. Hope is not a strategy or a goal. Dare her to make a plan to be in that store in a year. Ask her to make a commitment to getting that plan done. Promise her that if she wants someone to take a look at it, then you are available. And keep that promise. Find the time. It will, without any doubt, come back to you over and over again. Praise and encourage her as she works the plan. Celebrate progress together!

If a member of your team expresses frustration about a particular initiative, simply ask if they have developed a plan to get the work done. If they haven't, you now know what tools to pull from your coach leader toolbox to help them get moving. "Wait a minute! That's not my job! That's their boss's job to get them to plan." That's old thinking. Replace that thought with one that affirms your responsibility to help everyone to get ahead as a way of making your organization great. Take the lead. And keep it.

Coaching TO GO

1. **The power of focus**—One of the best templates that I have found for creating a plan to achieve more of what we want in our personal and professional lives can be found in a book entitled *The Power of Focus* by Jack Canfield and others. It also emphasizes the value of committing our goals to writing.

2. **You first!**—I have said this so often that it's practically a mantra. Nevertheless, preparing a plan to identify and achieve your own goals is simply a prerequisite for helping others to do the same. So, find a planning tool that "blows your skirt up" and use it for your own purposes. Engage in self-coaching and call on others around you to coach you along the way. It is the only

truly authentic way that I currently know to coach powerfully in this area.

3. **Craft some coaching questions/observations**—Create three to five coaching questions/observations that you might ask someone during the planning phase of goal work. Do the same thing for the implementation phase. Use your own language, but make sure that these questions and/or observations rise to the level of *powerful.*

4. **Situation analysis**—Take the challenge and work through the following typical organizational situation to refine your coaching ability around goal achievement:

    You have recently assumed the role of team leader in your organization. Marv is a member of your team. He has been a solid performer—he is neither performance challenged nor a performance star. You ask quite casually what his goals are for the coming year one day and are surprised by his answer: he doesn't have any specific goals. He likes his work to be organic and flow depending on the changing priorities of the environment, the organization, the boss, etc. Being nimble is one thing, you say to yourself, but being like a cork bobbing on the water, is entirely different. As a coach leader, how can you use the learning from this module on goal setting and achievement to help Marv lead from his seat?

5. **Build your own**—Now create your own situation analysis from your own experience or a current situation in your workplace. As always, use the space at the end of the chapter, get out your notebook or journal; or if you only can write at a keyboard, put the book down and go to the computer. Have fun and see if this doesn't open up a new way of seeing a potentially bad or harmful situation at work.

Advanced Coach Leader Behavior #6:

Playfulness—The Light Side of Leadership

Necessity may be the mother of invention,
but play is certainly the father.
—Roger von Oech

One of my treasured moments in Daniel Pink's book, *A Whole New Mind,* is when he tells his readers that to effectively prepare to make the shift into the Conceptual Age, and more importantly to thrive in it, we need to learn how to *play* at work. With play, he says, we can begin to cultivate a new and very different set of leadership aptitudes.[36]

Play is assuming an increasingly important role in work, business, learning, and personal well-being. It is showing up in the workplace in three primary ways: gaming, humor, and joyfulness.

I must confess that when, about four years ago an executive hired me as his coach/success partner to achieve the goal of experiencing more joy in his work, I almost fell out of my chair. It was an "aha!" moment for me. Business professionals were getting serious about playing more at work because they "got it"! They realized its legitimate value in creating a great place to work and in having extraordinary business results.

Play provides a portal to our creative selves. Cultivating it in ourselves and assisting those around us to do the same can have some powerful benefits:

- Games, particularly computer and video games, are becoming influential at work because they require players to engage both left and right brains—they create whole-brained thinkers! Research tells us that we learn quicker and retain more when games are involved.

- Humor is proving to be an accurate marker for leadership effectiveness, emotional intelligence, and relationship development. In the *Harvard Business Review*, Fabio Sala reported that humor reduces hostility, deflects criticism, relieves tension, improves morale, and greases the wheels of communication. This research also found that "the most effective leaders deployed humor twice as often as middle of the pack leaders." Humor has increasingly been recognized as an important glue that helps to create workplace community. [37]
- Not to be left behind, joy has the potential to make us more productive and fulfilled at work.

Think about it. When there is lightness or playfulness, aren't you more engaged in the work, in the discussion? Aren't you a better solution maker? More open and receptive? Keep in mind that most of us are at the creative high point in our lives around five years of age! Play helps us to reconnect with the five-year-old that is still tucked within us and takes advantage of the curiosity and creativity that flows so easily at that age.

It is little wonder, then, that as coach leaders we want to intentionally use play to help ourselves and others learn and grow. This is a specialized coaching skill and it requires an intuitive sense about when play is an appropriate tool. Let's be honest—we are all in serious business situations. And we need to be respectful of that. But sometimes we take ourselves entirely too seriously. There is also a time and place for play at work.

Many of us have lost our sense of experimentation, imagination, adventure, and freedom when it comes to the workplace. Many tell me that they feel heavy and weighed down most of the time at work. For this reason, using play as a strategic coaching tool is as much about unlearning as it is about learning.

Regularly incorporating playfulness in our work days allows us to recapture the lightness and openness of childhood. Professionals who have recaptured play demonstrate more innovation, more positive energy, greater measures of creative problem solving, and are generally better at work place relationships and creating community. They usually express more satisfaction and fulfillment with their work. I have some great resources to share with you in the Coaching TO GO section of this chapter.

Some common situations in which you can encourage yourself and others to play are:

- **Strategic thinking and planning**—Play taps into our genius and allows us to dream, to envision, and to create sparks of possibility. It also can be the catalyst for discovering the way forward, for developing the roadmap that will move us forward. Play refreshes and revitalizes our human spirit. It clears the mental cobwebs that can get in the way of clear, crisp thinking.

- **Problem solving mode**—Play relaxes the brain and frees up space that was occupied by stress and worry. Solutions that seemed evasive show up more effortlessly in the midst of play. Studies show that children who are allowed to daydream have higher IQs.

- **Work/life balance**—Achieving balance, not making more money, is the Number 1 concern of employees at all levels within organizations in the U.S. and Canada. The ability to feel happy on the job is positively influenced when play is a vital part of the workplace community.

- **High levels of frustration are early signs of burnout**—There is a Zen saying: "The bow that is forever taut will break." Play provides necessary breaks between the heavy lifting that we must do each day at work. It helps us relax and let go so that we do not hold on so tightly.

- **Attracting and keeping top talent**—Studies show a positive correlation between attracting, cultivating, and keeping top talent (particularly Generation X & Millennials) and having a creative, fun, and challenging workplace.

- **Overcoming a plateau or feeling stuck**—Play can be a marvelous tool for creating breakthroughs of all sorts, both individually and for teams.

Leading others through playfulness manifests itself, in my experience, in three general ways.

- **Act like a five year old**—Playing games, using toys and reading children's books are some of the ways that we can recapture the fun and spontaneity of just being a kid.

  When I visit a client site for the first time, I always am very attentive to how I feel when I first walk in the place. I remember one of those initial visits vividly because this particular organization had so artfully and so successfully woven play into their culture. When I walked in the front door, they were giving out those small bottles of bubbles. Everyone got one! Clients too. And throughout the day, throughout the building, I saw lots of people blowing bubbles and having a blast. I am not sure that I can think of another time when I saw more smiles in a day. The fun hung in the air. It felt good. You were glad that you were there and I personally was sad to leave. I was still chuckling to myself in the car as I drove away.

  Recently, one member of the purchasing department of a larger organization confided in me that the entire department had hula hoops that they periodically took out to play together. I think contests were involved. By the way, this particular purchasing department is a model of high team performance, has excellent relationships with other departments, and a track record of effective, error free service. Let the fun begin!

- **Jump starting imagination**—As we have learned together, and I am certain we are all experiencing, change is a business constant. It is an important part of who we are at work and what we do individually and together, to be consistently challenging same-old, same-old thinking and behaving. That means that we must look at our work with fresh eyes each day, looking for new and better ways of providing our service. In order to allow that to happen, we need to tap into our right brains and uncork the imagination genie in all of us. We need to practice a habit that I call non-stop innovation. Playfulness primes us to be open and receptive to that part of ourselves. Organizations that consistently show up on the Innovation Index have embedded practices within their cultures aimed at tapping into imagination to foster, creativity, invention, and innovation.

- **Fostering collaboration through games, contests, events, and volunteerism**—It is still so rewarding for me to experience just how spirited and animated individuals, teams, and entire organizations can be when connected through games, good natured contests, events, and service projects. Infusing this energy into our organizational cultures creates the WIN/WIN scenarios that we all want.

Now what? What can I do with my new understanding of play that will make a difference at work and help me to lead from my seat?

The information systems team at a large multi-state bank were one year into a two-year system overhaul. The hours were long. Internal and external customers were frustrated with the change process. The staff began to feel overwhelmed to the point of being paralyzed. Our left brains may tell us to press on and get the new system in place. We may ultimately be successful in getting that system in place that way. But the cost will be high. There may well be a string of burned out employees in its wake. There is another way that engaged cultures use strategically. Play. How about declaring victory for a portion of the initiative? And rewarding folks with a brief period of time off? Or change the channel. Get people thinking together differently. Maybe through a shared volunteer project, in which we use our hands and our hearts inside of our minds. Consider small rewards for team members. Encourage customers to share success stories and publish them. How about simply taking a lunch break for a change and eating together? Keep it simple. Laugh. Enjoy. It's refreshing and will lead to renewed engagement and dedication. Interestingly, such pauses never adversely impact the project schedule in my opinion!

Coaching TO GO

1. **Add to your professional library**—Anther must read for inspired use of play as a coaching tool is *You Don't Have to go Home from Work Exhausted* by Ann McGee-Cooper. The

workbook format of this delightful resource makes it both practical as well as valuable. Find creative ideas for taking energy breaks throughout the work day. Another stimulating book is *A Whack On The Side Of Your Head* by Roger von Eoch. Also try his companion tool, the Creative Whack Pack. It's a deck of cards that will most definitely whack you out of your thought ruts in a playful way.

2. **Take inspired action**—Think of three things that you can do readily at work to apply play and lightness as coaching approaches. Then do them!

3. **Bring out your (or someone else's) super hero**—I've already told you that I'm a fan of the old TV show *Xena Warrior Princess*. I am embarrassed to admit that I watched it regularly, but I did because I loved her sense of fun—and I loved those bracelets! I've already told you that Xena had these amazing bracelets that allowed her to deflect any weapon simply by raising her wrists. I often encourage my executive coaching clients to "get out their Xena bracelets" when it comes to deflecting gossip, negativity, destructive criticism, or other toxic weapon in the workplace. We both get a laugh out of it. We make the sounds of the bracelets coming into contact with the negativity and deflecting and laugh again. The client remembers to deflect because the reference to Xena made our conversation memorable and fun. It works! This is an example of using a super hero with super powers to help ourselves and others to create and sustain change. How can you bring out the super hero in us all? Using play as a coaching tool requires that you engage with your own creativity center: your right brain. This is one of those times when appearing to be silly is a good thing.

4. **Use games to reinforce learning**—Participants will retain more from learning programs if you use gaming as a tool. For example, I frequently use "Jeopardy" to highlight the key learning points and make them as sticky as possible. One of my organizational clients has used Civility Jeopardy to embed

the practice of civility, respect, and consideration in all interactions within the organization. We had so much fun creating the answers and developing the program. And it was universally well received—each program during their Education Fair was "sold out"! People want to learn and they want to have fun—"edu-tainment."

5. **Situation analysis**—Put your coach leader skill to the test with the following case study:

Laura is a Vice President with a large multinational corporation. She is about to be promoted to Senior Vice President. When she is promoted, she will be in charge of twice as many employees and projects as she is currently. She will also have ten more direct reports than she has now. She will also have to move to a new location. This promotion is a huge opportunity for Laura and she wants to take full advantage of it. She is concerned, however, because she already has trouble managing everything on her plate and now she will have twice as much. She has tried time management systems before, but they do not seem to work for her. She is also a great procrastinator. She wants help from you as her coach to make this promotion work and work well for both her and the company.

Describe three ways you might use play as a coaching tool with Laura.

Notes:

8

Putting It All Together

Coaching Conversation Pathways

"Don't put words in my mouth, I've got plenty to say..."
—President Barack Obama

Being a coach leader and leading from your seat in your organization requires that you are "on" every day and all the time. It is an amazing opportunity to be your best, authentic self because to be the most effective, you are always coaching and always willing to be coached. Every exchange with someone presents an opportunity to coach because every exchange with someone is a chance to communicate.

Because coach leadership has intentional communication at its core, there is room in this approach for lots of different styles and preferences. That's the art of it. I have just showered you with information, examples, and calls to action. You need to try each skill on for size and make it your own. Being someone different, doing different things, and shedding old habits is uncomfortable. That's a healthy part of professional growth.

As you regularly use these skills and experiment with them, they will fit you better and better until they become a part of your style and approach. However, in order to coach well, you must be your best self, not a fake. Not someone who puts on a mask at work and follows a script. Give yourself permission to take risks and not be perfect the first dozen times. It is okay to make a mistake! Simply learn from it. Look at what happened and what you could have done better—that's self-coaching, and there's never anything wrong with that!

Scripts to Get You Started

I realize that I have emphasized that our everyday conversations as a coach leader need to be genuine in order to be effective. Sometimes, though, getting started is the hardest part. As I have helped thousands of people in various types of organizations learn how to become effective coach leaders, I have found that providing them scripts to follow can really give them a way to jump into a coach position without fearing that they're going to mess up.

So, following that successful action, I have provided two scripts for you to either use as a way to think about how to incorporate coach leadership into your everyday interactions, or to actually sit down with someone and practice. Literally take one of the two personas that I have given you and say the words. You will be surprised at how helpful it is to actually form the words and the syntax of a coaching conversation from a script first before doing it on your own.

However, I do want to caution you. Many times people think of scripting as a prewritten conversation that must be followed closely. Some organizations effectively use scripts when changes in procedures are introduced, so that everyone can get used to a new way of doing things. Scripts are frequently used so that all members of a team share the same message with important groups, such as our customers, clients, or patients. And often-times, new team members benefit from the use of a script as they learn the details of their new business environment.

For me, following tightly prescribed scripts or having rigid checklists of questions to ask when becoming a coach leader is less beneficial because we are literally talking about a way of being in *every interaction throughout your day*. There is no script that can possibly cover that variety of conversations.

Leading from your seat truly requires genuineness and sincerity. We've got to find a way to be ourselves because it is part of what makes this approach so very effective. So, don't let me or anyone else put words in your mouth. I believe in you and your ability to take these skills, and, using examples, make them your very own.

One of my clients told me once that he occasionally felt like a ventriloquist's dummy when his boss told him what to say in certain situations. He jokingly said that he half expected his boss to put his hand up his back at key moments in a meeting and move this mouth for him!

So let me be clear. The following scripts are examples of coaching conversation pathways. These are intended to give you some sense of how natural the skills can be in everyday conversation, yet still deliver on the promise of full-throttle engagement and leaders at all levels and layers within the organization.

You will see when you read them that there isn't anything earth shattering about them. They really are everyday conversations. Use them to stimulate your own creativity.

I could hear something close to these examples in any organization on any given day. They are not right or wrong; they simply represent one way of using the skills of a coach leader to make a positive difference in everyday ways. There are no "announcements" about coaching. No need to pull out a script. Remember that most coach leader conversations are low key, everyday interactions that are artfully different from conversations you normally engaged in before taking this hero's journey.

Scenario #1—Colleague reacting to a change in procedure

Angela: Hey Beth, did you hear that we're going to have to change the way that we're doing our daily reporting starting on Monday?!?! Can't they leave anything alone? Can't we have a week where nothing changes? (Tone of voice seems to indicate frustration, anger, and/or blame)

Beth: (Pauses. Turns toward Angela, looks her in the eye, stops answering email messages and listens to her in a charge neutral way) I'm not sure I know exactly what you're talking about. Tell me a little more. (Uses active listening skill to prompt and clarify)

Angela: Well, now we have to use the new system and input all of our data directly into the online spreadsheet. We have to do it ourselves rather than having the clerk do it for us. It's going to take lots more time, that's for sure. And I hate that new system.

Beth: Okay, thanks for that clarification. Now I know what you're talking about. I heard about this change at staff meeting two weeks ago. Jonathan did a quick presentation on it. I remember you being there too, right?

Angela: Well, yeah, but it was a high-level summary and I didn't think it would be implemented so fast.

Beth: Okay, let's see if I've got this straight. You did know about the change but you didn't know the details and the timeframe for implementation. Is that right? (Actively reflecting back and clarifying.)

Angela: I suppose so.

Beth: I'm remembering that Jonathan made a point of reminding us that this change was a recommendation from the Quality Improvement Committee. Do you remember that the same way I do?

Angela: Yeah, I guess.

Beth: What's your take on the work that Committee is doing? (Coaching inquiry.)

Angela: I think they've been doing some great work and we really seem to be making progress toward certification since that committee got rolling.

Beth: I really agree with you. They are awesome. The members are dedicated and they often ask for input on different issues. I trust them. (Pause.)

Angela: Now that you say that, I actually do remember seeing something from them about a Q&A (question and answer) session on the new system and some administrative changes that would be made as a result. I was so busy I didn't pay much attention to it last month. Maybe I wouldn't be so upset if I had gone and shared my reservations with them at that time. But it's just too late now.

Beth: Is it? (Pause. Practice silence. Ask a coaching question to challenge assumptions. Is it really too late to offer input or share some concerns?)

Angela: Is it what?

Beth: Is it true that it is too late to share some of your concerns? (Truth seeking. Powerful coaching question that challenges same-old, same-old thinking)

Angela: Well, I'm just assuming that since it's been implemented that they aren't interested anymore?

Beth: That may or may not be true. I tend to think that they want to hear from people on a regular basis. (Truth telling. Challenging assumptions.) What if they're interested in keeping the lines of communication open of this particular change? What if they want all of us to share our thoughts with them? What if they can help you to learn more about the new system so that you wouldn't hate it going forward? ("What if upping.")

Angela: Do you think it would be worth it to talk to them, maybe go to their next meeting?

Beth: What do you think? (The four most powerful words in a workplace conversation… followed by silence.)

Angela: I'm thinking it's worth a try and probably better than just griping about it.

Beth: Cool. I agree. One thing that I have always appreciated about you is that you can put yourself in someone else's shoes. (Identifying brilliances. Building someone) You mentioned earlier that our clerks used to do this work for us. It feels to me as though they have become overwhelmed with more and more work and this change might be an opportunity to give them some breathing room. You were in that position at one time. How do you think that they are viewing this change?

Angela: (thinking) They're probably relieved. They really have been life savers this past year, in getting that backlog taken care of. They also may be able to lend a hand to those of us who are less familiar with the system.

Beth: I have found them to be really willing to help me find short-cuts on the new system. They're good people. I keep reminding myself that we are all in this together.

Angela: You know, you have a point. Maybe this is more about my own fear of the new technology and less about who does what with the data.

Beth: That's a good insight on your part. Now, when are you planning to reach out to the QI Committee? Please touch base with me and let me know how things go. (Checking resolve and commitment. Planning. Goal setting with timeline.)

Angela: I think the meeting is next Tuesday over lunch. I'll send you an email afterward.

Scenario #2—Two Colleagues Discussing Third Person

Dan: Katherine really gets under my skin! She **never** pulls her weight around here. I can't stand to be on the shift with her. In fact, when Jeff asked if I could work on Saturday, I told him no because I would be teamed up with Katherine. (makes a face.)

Marj: (pause to gather thoughts) You sound really upset and frustrated. That's rare for you. I usually can count on you to be positive and constructive and a really creative problem solver. (Identifies signature strengths & personal care and builds individual.) Why is this situation different?

Dan: I don't really know. It may not be logical but I just get annoyed when I'm around her. I think I'm going to take this to Jeff and ask him to talk to her about doing her fair share of the work.

Marj: Have you spoken directly to Katherine to share your feelings with her and work together on a solution? (Coaching question, collaborative inquiry.)

Dan: No, I doubt that she would be receptive and anyway, that's not my job. (Hands folded across chest.)

Marj: Dan, how is that approach consistent with coach leadership and our rules of engagement here? (Coaching question.)

Dan: What do you mean?

Marj: We have agreed to treat each other as adults and with respect and civility. We also agreed to accept personal responsibility for having good, strong relationships with each other. We all lead from our seats, remember?

Dan: Yeah (rolls eyes). I know what you're going to say next!

Marj: What's that?

Dan: That I should talk to Katherine first. That I should give her the benefit of the doubt. And that maybe I should focus on the positive things about her instead of only the things that bug me.

Marj: Right on! You know what the right thing to do is. Is it possible that Katherine doesn't even know that she is bugging you or that she may not be doing her fair share of the work? Is it possible? (Coaching question.)

Dan: Maybe.

Marj: Is it really true that she isn't doing her part? (Sorting out the truths, challenging conclusions with a simple question.)

Dan: Well, I think it is.

Marj: I've had a different experience. I've worked successfully with Katherine. She has a crazy sense of humor and she is very social. And my take is that she really wants to do a great job but sometimes misses the mark on what that is. She's been really receptive to my constructive feedback and has given me permission to stop her if she is veering off course. (Affirming Katherine, truth telling, challenging assumptions.)

Dan: Well, maybe she's just sucking up to you or something.

Marj: (firm but charge neutral voice) I have no evidence that this is the case. Dan, I need to take a risk here and give you some feedback. I see it as my responsibility because we are such good colleagues and I do care about you and our team. It seems to me that you are choosing to think the worst of Katherine, with little or no evidence. (Coaching observation.) I've seen you be an amazing coach leader at times (affirming and building) so that makes me even more puzzled by your comments and tone of voice. Your words and your body language are sending me the message that you want me to agree with you or join in the complaining. (Coaching observation.) I'm choosing not to do that. (Intentionality.) It won't help the situation and it's not my honest opinion. (Silence for a moment.) What's your reaction to what I just said?

Dan: I'm surprised (looks surprised, more subdued). Was I really that bad?

Marj: Let me clarify my point (clarifying). You weren't your best self in this conversation so far. So let's make a course correction together and get moving in another, more constructive direction. What's one concrete thing that you can do that could help Katherine do a better job here and allow you to feel less frustrated? (Challenging, action oriented question, goal setting.)

Dan: (thinking) I could talk to her one on one to get to know her better and maybe ask her how things are going for her in the department.

Marj: That seems like a place to start. You may find out that you didn't have the whole story when you drew your conclusions. (Assuming partiality.) Are you making a commitment to having this conversation? (Checking on intent and resolve.)

Dan: Yes, actually, I am.

Marj: Cool. When? (Offering accountability.)

Dan: We work together tomorrow. Maybe we can have coffee together. You said that she was social, so maybe that would put her at ease and we can have a really good discussion.

Marj: Nice idea. So then, you're choosing to reach out to Katherine tomorrow and spend a few minutes with her over a cup of coffee at break. Did I hear that correctly?

Dan: That's my plan.

Marj: Let me know how things go. I care about both of you.

See how easy it is? Oh, and as you find yourself getting more comfortable with the flow of a coaching conversation, consider what some of my clients have done. They have created a "bank" of coaching conversation pathways and share them broadly within their organization in order to develop greater mastery and best practices. Maybe you and your team will choose to do the same. Please feel free to share them with me if you want to pass them along for use in the larger workplace community.

Coaching Conversation Framework

Now that you've seen and hopefully practiced coach leadership in action, I want to invite you to go back through the two conversations and see if you can identify a framework at play.

I just asked you to do this because I actually had one of my clients sit down with me and help me figure that out. Together we developed a very basic framework or structure for a coaching conversation pathway. I invite you to study it, both for its own merit and in conjunction with the scripts I just provided. It could be some of the most important work you do in this book for many reasons: sometimes we forget that many people have not had the chance to learn how to participate fully in a meaningful adult conversation; maybe that was just not their family's dynamic; or perhaps other workplace experiences didn't offer education or hold an expectation of full-throttle engagement.

Don't make the dangerous and often incorrect assumption that we all know how to talk to one another in a way that helps. Here is my simple guidance for how to begin to create new conversation habits, one conversation at a time:

Pause—Intentionally stop for a brief moment before you jump into a conversation. Gather your thoughts. Thirty seconds is all you need most of the time. Be aware. Be intentional. Get ready to listen. Be fully present.

Listen—We have learned that of all the things that we can do to help others feel valued and to set the stage for an effective interaction, that none more vital than to clearly listen. Use your coaching ear as much as possible.

Engage—Connect heart, head, and gut and be a coach leader in that moment. Be civil, respectful, and considerate. Choose to think the best of the situation. Come at it from a mindset of what's possible.

Ask—Remember how important it is to ask the person(s) questions so that you can understand more and to be helpful to that person as they refine and clarify their own thinking. It's okay to advocate for your position as well, as long as there is a balance. Don't forget that our questions can be provocative and challenging. We really want to get ourselves and others thinking differently.

Search for solutions together—Through asking (collaborative inquiry), begin to identify some possible ways to solve the issue, take advantage of the opportunity, resolve a conflict, etc.

Enhance together—Through an exchange of ideas, mind-storming, play, visioning, and synergy, make those possible solutions even better. Weed out the ones that won't fit without personally attacking someone for their idea.

Summarize—I know that it is tempting to just run off to your next task or your next meeting, thinking that summarizing isn't necessary. It is too easy for even well-intended colleagues to misunderstand something that happened in the conversation or come to very different conclusions from one another. Summarizing briefly can help.

Notes:

9 Epilogue:

The Glory Work

Congratulations! You have stuck with me throughout to find out how you can lead from your seat. You are my hero! Better yet, you are an organizational hero.

I want you to know something important. You have completed this hero's journey. You bravely set out on an adventure when you began turning the pages of this book or fired up your Kindle. You have traveled through an amazing landscape of possibility, a landscape that includes knowing that:

- The old-school way of leading is over.
- Everyone can and should lead from their seat each day at work.
- Full-throttle engagement isn't simply an organizational fairy tale, it's actually who we were meant to be at work and what we were meant to have; and it's what will help us to be successful and happy in the future
- Having full-throttle engagement and leading from our seats isn't something that is bestowed on us but rather something that each of us gets to choose simply by intentionally choosing our thoughts, feelings, words, attitudes, and behaviors each day.
- Being a coach leader is THE systematic way to lead from our seats and experience full-throttle engagement.
- The sooner we begin, each and every one of us, to be coach

leaders at work, the sooner we can ramp up to full engagement together and the sooner we will experience that fulfillment, satisfaction, and success that we all want.

You have successfully completed the hero's challenge of learning a new set of leadership thoughts and behaviors. The hero's prize is a new you. More now than ever, you are a VIL, a very important leader. Not because of your title or your tenure or your salary, but because every day you *do more than expected from your seat to help your colleagues, customers, and organization.*

But it is important to understand deeply that this hero's journey is a never-ending one. We never get the work of being a coach leader completely done. Even though we have gained new wisdom and activated new thoughts and behaviors, there will always be more to learn, more to refine, more to enhance.

And that, dear colleagues, is *"the glory work."* If you have taken this work into your head and your heart and taken full advantage of all of the learning, the growing, and the Coaching TO GO practical applications and exercises offered during this journey, then you have installed the major elements of a whole new approach to "work." That's worth celebrating.

Now you must sustain it, even during difficult moments, and you have to become even more artful and skillful going forward. Recalling the quote from Lizbeth Moss Cantor, sometimes this change will look like and feel like failure as you move through it. Heroes are courageous! Push past your fear and occasional discouragement or frustration.

What is glory work? It was coined by an everyday leader, Joyce Ross, the mother of my editor and publisher, Patricia Ross. For Joyce "glory work" is part of her house-cleaning ritual. It's the finishing work that you do after all the deep cleaning—the scrubbing, vacuuming, disinfecting, if necessary—is done. It's the dusting and putting everything back in order so that it looks amazing, inviting; and it feels good because even the corners have been cleaned out, everything is organized, and everything is shiny and pretty.

Epilogue

Patricia said that cleaning sometimes looked like a god-awful mess when Joyce did it. Everything was torn up, piles were everywhere. Even in the face of that challenge, she moved from one pile to the next, keeping the end result in her mind and handling everything until she knew that it was done to the very best of her ability. When she got to the "glory work" it really was deserving of great praise and distinction (the definition of glory).

How does this cleaning story relate to leading from your seat? For me, the learning from this cleaning story is this:

- You get the big stuff handled first.
- It can look like and feel like a real mess at times, but you press on and keep your eye on where you want to be and how good it will feel to be there.
- It's not enough, though, to just do the big stuff. You've got to refine and do lots of little stuff to make it the best.
- It's worth it. Doing the extra "little stuff" is the difference between good and great. It's the small, ongoing changes that create magic and are deserving of praise and distinction.

Gear up for the glory work of coach leadership. Break through difficult times. Continue to make small changes. Read the book again, do every single exercise offered, ask better questions, listen deeper, be more intentional, speak your truth more elegantly, lead from your seat even if it isn't the norm or hip or popular yet in your organization.

To paraphrase one line from a Lady Gaga song: "You're on the edge of glory and you're hanging on a moment of truth."

So in the grand tradition of coaching, I will leave you with one final powerful question from me to you:

"Is *your* seat a power seat?"

(Silence.)

NOTES

[1] Benjamin Zander and Rosamund Stone Zander. *The Art of Possibility.* New York: Penguin Books, 2002. Pages 68-70.

[2] Benjamin Zander and Rosamund Stone Zander , *The Art Of Possibility* (New York, NY: Penguin Books, 2002) Page. 76.

[3] Steve Crabtree. "Getting Personal in the Workplace," *The Gallop Management Journal* as it appears online at GovLeaders.org. Page 1.

[4] Dan Crim and Gerard Seijts. "What Engages Employees the Most or the Ten C's of Employee Engagement." *The Workplace.* March/April 2006. Page 1.

[5] Jamie Showkeir, Maren Showkeir and Margaret J. Wheatley. *Authentic Conversations: Moving from Manipulation to Truth and Commitment.* San Francisco: Berrett-Koehler Publishers, 2008. Forward by Margaret J Wheatley. Page xi.

[6] Benjamin Zander and Rosamund Stone Zander. *The Art of Possibility.* New York: Penguin Books, 2002.

[7] Tom Peters Video – *The Problem Isn't the Problem.. www.TomPeters.com*

[8] Lampton, Bill Ph.D., "My Pleasure – The Ritz Carlton Hotel Part II," Expert Magazine.com, 1999-2003.

[9] Buffalo Springfield, one of the most influential bands of the 1960s, was comprised of some of the great legends of rock and roll: Neil Young, Steven Stills, Jim Messina, and Richie Furay, all American Rock and Roll Hall of Fame musicians, singers, and songwriters. The original band performed from 1966 to 1968, and is most remembered for its song "For What It's Worth," written by Steven Stills.

[10] Malcolm Gladwell. *The Tipping Point: How Little Things Can Make A Big Difference.* New York: Back Bay Books (Little, Brown), 2002.

[11] Daniel Pink. *A Whole New Mind.* New York: Riverhead Books, 2005.

[12] Christopher J Hegarty and Philip B Nelson. *7 Secrets of Exceptional Leadership.* Mechanicsburg, PA: Executive Books. 1997. Page 36.

[13] Rodd Wagner and James K Harter. *12: The Elements of Great Managing.* New York: Gallop Press, 2006. Pages ix-xvii.

[14] Adapted with permission from Annette M. Cremo, President, Performance Plus Training & Consulting .

[15] Mark Victor Hansen and Robert G. Allen. *The One Minute Millionaire.* New York: Harmony Books, 2002. Page 20.

[16] McGovern, Ph.D., Michael Lindemann, Ph.D., Monica Vergara, M.A., Stacey Murphy, Linda Barker, M.A., & Rodney Warrenfeltz, Ph.D., "Maximizing the Impact of Executive Coaching: Behavioral Change, Organizational Outcomes, and Return on Investment," The Manchester Review, Vol. 6, No 1.

[17] Behavioral Coaching Institute. http://www.1to1coachingschool.com/ articlesnews.htm. ©1998-2008.

[18] Thomas G, Crane. *The Heart of Coaching* (San Diego, CA: FTA Press, 2005. Page 39.

[19] Jim Collins. *Good to Great.* New York: HarperCollins. 2001. Page 1.

[20] Stephen R. Covey. *The 7 Habits of Highly Effective People.* New York: Fireside. 1990. Pages 81-82

[21] Stephen R. Covey. *The 7 Habits of Highly Effective People.* New York: Fireside. 1990. Page 95.

[22] Mike Murdock. *The Leadership Secrets of Jesus.* Fort Worth, TX: The Wisdom Center.

[23] Joe Vitale. *Spiritual Marketing.* First Books Library, 2001.

[24] Benjamin Zander and Rosamund Stone Zander. *The Art of Possibility.* New York: Penguin Books, 2002. Page 125.

[25] Benjamin Franklin. *The Autobiography of Benjamin Franklin.* New Haven, CT: Yale University Press, 1964. Pages 149-152.

[26] Adapted with permission from Annette M. Cremo, President, Performance Plus Training & Consulting.

[27] Tom Peters Video. "Listening." www.TomPeters.com.

[28] Wayne W Dyer, Ph.D. *The Power of Intention.* Carlsbad, CA: Hay House, Inc. 2004.

[29] PM Forni. *Choosing Civility: The 25 Rules of Considerate Conduct.* New York: St. Martin's Griffin, 2003.

[30] Jamie Showkeir and Maren Showkeir. *Authentic Conversations: Moving from Manipulation to Truth and Commitment.* San Francisco: Berrett-Koehler Publishers, 2008.

[31] "Margaret Mead." Wikipedia. http://en.wikiquote.org/wiki/Margaret_Mead.

[32] Kurt Wright. *Breaking The Rules.* Boise, ID: CPM Publishing, 1998. Pages 39-40.

[33] Deborah Ancona, Thomas W Malone, Wanda J Orlinski and Peter Senge. "In Praise of the Incomplete Leader," *Harvard Business Review, February 2007. Pages 110-117.*

[34] Tom Peters. *Re-imagine* London, England: Dorling Kindersley, 2003

[35] Stephen R. Covey. *The 7 Habits of Highly Effective People.* New York: Fireside. 1990. Page 95.

[36] Daniel Pink. *A Whole New Mind.* New York: Riverhead Books, 2005

[37] Fabio Sala. "Laughing All the Way to the Bank." *Harvard Business Review.* Sept. 2003. http://hbr.org/2003/09/laughing-all-the-way-to-the-bank/ar/1.

About the Author

THE WOMAN YOU NEED
FOR TODAY'S BUSINESS TRANSFORMATION

Leta Beam is one of the most powerful and energetic voices for business transformation in the twenty-first century, sharing her message of full throttle engagement and leadership from every seat through coaching, teaching, speaking, entertaining and writing.

Leta is President of Vantage International, a premier leadership and business coaching enterprise, dedicated to serving high performing professionals and organizations using a dynamic, results oriented coaching system called AdVantage. The AdVantage Coaching System challenges clients to view themselves as powerful forces in their own lives and the lives of their organizations. It offers a unique blend of intentional thinking and laser-focused action steps that delivers significant bottom line results.

One of her brilliances is helping others to "get on a roll" and stay there. Whether coaching one-to-one with high performing professionals around the world or one-to-many with professional teams, groups. committees, entire businesses, boards of trustees or broad business audiences, Leta's framework is the same: each of us is a powerful force in our own experience, if we choose to be. In order for us to improve our conditions, then, we must intentionally change, not because we are told to or because someone manages, directs, cajoles or browbeats us. Rather, through our own will. Sustainable shifts are intentional and self-induced. Every seat is a power seat!

Not everyone is ready to open the throttle up and put the pedal to the metal. Yet Leta creates a safe space in which others can think about things differently and every voice can be heard. Her infectious energy helps those around her to believe that everything is possible and inspires them to more actively engage at work.

Leta works at every level from executives to management to team members, entrepreneurs and small business owners and across different industries and disciplines. Leta partners with companies throughout the world such as: AHOLD/Giant Foods, Bassett Healthcare Network, Coldwell Banker, Commonwealth of Pennsylvania, KPMG, Lifespan, Planned Parenthood, Ritchey Engineering, and SYMMCO. (For a full list of clients please visit www.vantage-inter.com.

Above all, Leta is recognized for an engaging style and fresh, results-oriented messages. She is the author of numerous articles on healthcare, managed care and, most recently, business coaching, leadership, personal mastery and business excellence. In front of both national and international audiences, "Leta...leaves them (the audience) changed." You can really have it all in one presentation! - Informational and transformational learning; humor and challenge; sparks of possibility. Leta has been featured in newspaper and journal articles as the "energetic woman who can beat psychosclerosis (hardening of the attitudes)."

Leta shares a home with her husband, Jim, in Central Pennsylvania that is playfully called, "La La Land." Leta was recognized as one of the "Best 50 Women In Business in PA." She has appeared in a calendar, titled "Portraits of Strength" for Pinnacle Health System in Central PA. And she was selected as one of the fittest CEOs in Central PA. She is adjunct faculty at her alma mater, Penn State University, where she designs and delivers leadership curricula. Leta is also an adjunct professor at Saint Francis University, where she offers MBA courses in coaching, creating workplace community and talent planning.

She is a bicyclist, ballroom dancer, exercise enthusiast and, most significantly, a lover of life.

An Invitation to Connect

Please consider this Leta Beam's personal invitation to contact her to explore how she can more fully support you and your organization's journey to

Full-throttle Engagement!

To lead from your seat and take advantage of this invitation, please contact us at Vantage International:

717-238-3939

leta@vantage-inter.com

How Good Can You Stand It?